Drama 3–5: A practical guide to teaching drama to children in the foundation stage

How can you promote creative and active learning in an early years setting to fill young children with confidence and enthusiasm?

The importance of using drama to support the learning of young children is increasingly recognised in a wide range of pre-school settings. Young children participating in well-taught and planned drama activities will develop strong social skills, more self-confidence and a deep understanding of co-operation and team-work.

Drama 3–5 gives early years practitioners the tools they need to offer children frequent opportunities to express themselves and develop these invaluable life-skills.

Based on the extensive tried and tested experience of the author, this highly practical book shows early years practitioners how to teach drama and stagework to children from 3–5 years. The wide variety of accessible activities and sample session plans are set alongside intended learning objectives of the Foundation Stage in chapters looking at

- building confidence and social skills
- mime and expression
- movement and dance
- speech and language
- rhythm and singing
- safety and teamwork

Drama 3–5 prepares early years practitioners to lead and develop dramatic work with confidence and enthusiasm, whilst ensuring they understand the theory and the value behind each activity. Any early years practitioner who wants to make drama a really fun and enjoyable activity with their children will find this book an invaluable companion.

Debbie Chalmers is a drama teacher, freelance drama consultant and a regular contributor to *Nursery World* and the *TES*.

The Nursery World/Routledge Essential Guides for Early Years Practitioners

Books in this series, specially commissioned and written in conjunction with *Nursery World* magazine, address key issues for early years practitioners working in today's nursery and school environments. Each title is packed full of practical activities, support, advice and guidance, all of which is in line with current government early years policy. The authors use their experience and expertise to write accessibly and informatively, emphasising through the use of case studies the practical aspects of the subject, whilst retaining strong theoretical underpinnings throughout.

These titles will encourage the practitioner and student alike to gain greater confidence and authority in their day-to-day work, offering many illustrative examples of good practice, suggestions for further reading and many invaluable resources. For a handy, clear and inspirational guide to understanding the important and practical issues, the early years practitioner or student need look no further than this series.

Titles in the series:

Circle Time for Young Children
Jenny Mosley

Developing Positive Behaviour in the Early Years
Sue Roffey

Identifying Additional Learning Needs in the Early Years: listening to the children
Christine MacIntyre

Understanding Children's Development in the Early Years: questions practitioners frequently ask
Christine MacIntyre

Observing, Assessing and Planning for Children in the Early Years
Sandra Smidt

Encouraging Creative Play and Learning in the Early Years (forthcoming)
Diane Rich

Essential Nursery Management: A practitioner's guide (forthcoming)
Susan Hay

Learning and Playing Outdoors (forthcoming)
Jan White

Thinking and Learning about Maths in the Early Years (forthcoming)
Linda Pound

Drama 3–5

A practical guide to teaching drama to children in the foundation stage

Debbie Chalmers

Routledge
Taylor & Francis Group
LONDON AND NEW YORK

NURSERY WORLD

First published 2007
by Routledge
2 Park Square, Milton Park, Abingdon, Oxon OX14 4RN

Simultaneously published in the USA and Canada
by Routledge
270 Madison Ave, New York, NY 10016

Routledge is an imprint of the Taylor & Francis Group, an informa business

Typeset in Perpetua and Bell Gothic by
Florence Production Ltd, Stoodleigh, Devon
Printed and bound in Great Britain by
MPG Books Ltd, Bodmin

British Library Cataloguing in Publication Data
A catalogue record for this book is available from the British Library

Library of Congress Cataloging in Publication Data
A catalog record for this book has been requested

ISBN10: 0–415–42168–3 (hbk)
ISBN10: 0–415–42169–1 (pbk)
ISBN10: 0–203–96216–8 (ebk)

ISBN13: 978–0–415–42168–3 (hbk)
ISBN13: 978–0–415–42169–0 (pbk)
ISBN13: 978–0–203–96216–9 (ebk)

Contents

Chapter 1

A good beginning

Young children are naturally dramatic. They learn about the world and make sense of their experiences through acting out scenes and characters in their play. If you watch and listen to them in the role play area or with 'small world' figures, you will see how they choose and develop characters, try them out, enjoy them and then discard them in favour of the next game.

Some children naturally play in this way from a very young age, often because they have been encouraged to do so at home with their family. Others learn to do it by copying and joining in with their peers. Some find this type of play more challenging or do not choose it spontaneously. A good early years practitioner will help and support them in this area and offer suitable opportunities for dramatic play to develop, being aware of the enormous educational and social benefits for all children.

The inclusion of group drama sessions within the foundation stage enriches the curriculum for all children and staff. However, some practitioners do not recognise that very young children are able and ready to participate in organised drama at an appropriate level, and many do not feel confident enough to lead group sessions in this area. Those who do wish to bring more drama into their planning may have to convince colleagues that sessions will be of value and also that they will be enjoyable.

The suggestions and activities in this book can be used by all childcare and education professionals who wish to lead drama sessions with children aged 3 to 5. They are equally suitable for use in a day nursery, pre-school or playgroup or in a nursery or reception class in a state or independent school. Each activity may be shortened, lengthened, adapted or extended to match the needs of the children taking part. Sessions may be planned to specifically target the age group contained within one class or to be flexible enough to accommodate a group of children of mixed ages. It should also be possible to make links with other areas of learning and to make available opportunities for appropriate imaginative and role play for those children who choose to extend their drama experiences.

Drama for young children can encompass every area of the foundation stage curriculum. As well as the obvious creative, physical and communication skills that children develop through sharing drama activities, their mathematical development and knowledge and understanding of the world can be easily stimulated through the choice of appropriate songs and stories and imaginative use of space. But it is in the areas of personal, social and emotional development that many young children gain the most, as they grow in confidence and self-esteem and learn to work together with others. Even the shyest child or one with very little social experience will enjoy singing or dance or making expressions or joining in with stories within a group, when s/he does not feel that anyone is looking to judge or compare. And children learn best when they are enjoying themselves.

With the right equipment, a well-planned programme, some good ideas, confidence, flexibility and lots of enthusiasm, an early years practitioner can make a valuable extra contribution to children's development – while they find out that drama is fun!

BEFORE EACH SESSION

Allow time to set up your equipment and prepare your space. Ensure that the room you are using is cleared of all furniture and toys that could present a safety risk or a distraction. Children will only appreciate drama as an activity in its own right if they are encouraged to move around and concentrate on stories and songs in a large, clear space. There should be no danger of them bumping into tables and chairs or looking longingly at rows of inviting toys on shelves or on the floor!

When children first come together to begin a drama session, they need to feel that they are all equally important and valued within the group and that others are pleased that they have come. Confident, talkative children will want their teacher to listen to their latest news or answer their questions, while quieter children may just be hoping that you will notice their toy or new T-shirt or hairstyle. Others may not yet wish to be the centre of attention at any time or may even be wearing a very attractive garment that they happen to dislike. The aim here is to comment on the right things and ignore the right ones – this gets easier with practice, but nobody gets it right every time!

Through your day to day conversations with parents, carers and colleagues, you will know when a child is feeling particularly tired or fragile, excited or very energetic, coping with an upheaval or trauma or

Figure 1 Children need comfortable clothes and shoes, and a floor surface that is safe and clean.

disappointed that their best friend is absent. Background information enables you to make allowances for certain behaviours, accept that a child is temporarily making slower progress, or offer extra support or extra challenges and stimulation to ensure that children can derive maximum benefit from each session. Everybody involved should be able to look forward to sessions as a time to get together and learn while having fun.

Check that the floor is safe and clean enough to work on. Remember that you may want to include activities such as sliding like a caterpillar or pretending to ice skate, crawling on hands and knees like an animal or rolling in imaginary mud or leaves. It would be unusual to find a nursery with an unsafe floor surface, but some playgroups, for example, may share the use of a hall with a wooden floor. Children should always wear shoes if there is any danger of splinters and never just slippery socks or tights to dance on a polished floor.

Carpet is not the best floor surface for drama activities, as it does not allow satisfying sounds when stamping and jumping and can harbour dust which could affect allergic children when their faces are close to it, but it is safe and can be used if there is no alternative. Ask staff to vacuum the carpeted area just before your arrival to ensure cleanliness and safety, and to allow dust time to settle before each session. If using a hard floor surface, ensure that it will not be too cold or too warm for children to stand, sit and lie on and remind the children at each session that they must take especial care not to fall over and bump their heads.

MAINTAINING RELATIONSHIPS

As you will need to prepare your drama sessions in advance, ensure that colleagues understand the importance of sticking to the times you have agreed and giving the full length of time promised to each session. Settings offering part-time sessions to their children must follow the timetable that works for them and complete each activity before the children are collected. Those offering full daycare will also have a structured routine of activities, playtimes, meals and rest periods that they need to adhere to.

Agree with colleagues how long each group of children is likely to be able to concentrate on and enjoy drama activities, maybe starting with slightly shorter sessions and gradually building up to longer ones if this is their first experience of drama.

The staff team should make time to chat with each other for a few moments at the beginning and end of each session. It is always good for the children to see that all of the adults in their setting get on well with each other, respect each other and work consistently for the good of the group. A friendly relationship will ensure that both you and they feel happy to raise and discuss any areas of potential concern before they become problems. In this way difficulties can be minimised or prevented. Key workers will feel able to seek each other's advice on identifying areas where extra support may benefit a child. You will be able to offer each other valuable insights into a child's behaviour and abilities, to record and confirm areas of progress and celebrate achievements. This may be particularly helpful for children with special needs.

Some children who appear to struggle in many areas or to be unable to overcome their shyness or to communicate with others can 'find a voice' and thrive through exploring drama. Others find it a good area for channelling their energies and demonstrating their creative potential, showing concentration and imaginative skills previously undiscovered in other activities.

If you share your lesson plans with all of the staff in your setting, they will be more able to support your teaching and also able to develop possible extension activities for children who have enjoyed the themes they worked on in drama. Offering a few weeks of lesson plans at a time, in advance, may facilitate the best co-operative working between you.

Staff may choose to take turns to accompany children to their drama sessions, or those who enjoy it most may take on the task most regularly. You may also find that you are asked to include students, volunteers or junior staff who will learn valuable skills through participating in your sessions. It will then be necessary to have realistic expectations of their abilities and to take pleasure in their developing skills and confidence along with the children's, but do make it clear from the very beginning that all adults must participate fully and encourage all children to join in and work to the best of their abilities. Enthusiasm and co-operation are the most important skills for them to maintain throughout. Talking to each other about unrelated topics, displaying embarrassment when acting or singing and allowing children to 'opt out' and sit on their laps to watch (unless you consider that a child has a real need to do this) are not acceptable!

In a nursery, pre-school, playgroup or school setting, children will have arrived and settled in before their drama class begins, so they will all arrive in the room as a group at the agreed time. It is important to greet all children and staff warmly and indicate that you are pleased to see that

Figure 2 Encourage the children to start each session with happy, smiling faces.

they are all ready for their drama session. Suitable opening comments might be:

> I'm so pleased to see that you are ready with such happy smiling faces.
>
> I was glad when I remembered it was Tuesday today, because it's our drama day.
>
> Isn't it lovely to have this room all ready for us to use for dancing, acting and singing?
>
> I've brought my special bag of things for us to look at later.
>
> I remember how good you all were at being cats last week, and I was excited to think about which animals we might be today.

Chapter 2

Warming up

You will need to indicate that your session is about to officially begin in an obvious way. This may involve asking for the staff and children's help in clearing a working space, by tidying away a previous activity and moving any furniture and equipment that could be a safety risk or a distraction factor, or letting colleagues know that you have prepared the equipment and the space and that they should now bring the children to the room.

Encourage everybody to come together and sit comfortably in a circle, checking that every child can see and be seen by you and the other members of the group. Ensure that all children have enough space and will be able to use their bodies without bumping each other or feeling cramped. It doesn't matter how big the circle grows – just encourage children to shuffle outwards a bit more and a bit more until they all have room! Take any child who benefits from extra support to sit beside you at first, or ensure that they are beside their key worker or another appropriate member of staff, but do this in a subtle manner. Never allow sitting beside you or another adult to become a status symbol or a source of competition or rivalry between children, or somebody will inevitably become unhappy.

To start a session in a happy way and put everybody into a constructive and co-operative mood, you can use an action song. The song chosen may be familiar to the children or completely new, but it needs to be cheerful and invite enthusiastic joining-in.

If you begin with the same song at each session, even the youngest child will come to associate it with the situation and the type of activities that follow and everybody will soon be in the right mood to work on drama.

Make sure that you choose a song that you think the adults will also enjoy, as they may need to model the correct level of enthusiasm and participation for some children at first. For this reason, it may be best to avoid the songs that appear most frequently on every children's tape and CD and are the 'standard diet' at nurseries, pre-schools, playgroups and toddler groups. Children do need to know these songs, but you should try to make your sessions a little more special.

Changing the song that you use as your 'opening number' each half-term or six weeks allows a good balance between the safe and familiar and the new challenge. But you should be prepared to be flexible about this. If you know that the children and the adults are still enjoying working on a song that was brand new to them only a few weeks ago, stay with it. But, if you sense that children or adults are becoming bored with one that they all know well, introduce a new one, or alternate between two or three for a while, so that nobody knows exactly which one it will be on a particular day.

Most importantly, ensure that you choose 'opening numbers' that you like and feel totally confident to deliver and lead. If you are a singer, feel free to display this ability.

Use songs that fit your range and preferred type of singing and 'perform' the number as you would before an audience. Others feel inspired to join in with this type of performance and often surprise themselves. If you are aware that your singing ability is more limited, select songs that allow you to lead through speech and actions and let the tape or CD carry the tune.

First impressions are very important. At any session, you may have at least one child and/or adult who has never attended before and they will not benefit very much until they start enjoying themselves and wanting to participate. Remember that it is much easier to achieve a downward spiral than an upward one, so you want everybody to begin 'on a high' and stay there as long as possible before coming down gradually, rather than trying to climb up as a session progresses. Keep more difficult or less exciting work for the middle of a session.

While children are fairly new to you, you may want to move quickly into your first song with little introduction, but, if you know them well, your relationship will often benefit from some 'standing jokes' and 'pretend mistakes'. Speak to the seated circle as a whole group and allow any child to answer you if they wish to. You may want to begin with phrases such as:

Have you all brought your hands today?
Did anybody bring their feet?
Let's give our mouths a wriggle to warm them up!

Then move on to:

How many hands have you brought?
We need these! What are they? (touching your ears)
Is your face ready? Feel it carefully to make sure it's all there!

And work up to:

Now everybody needs their three legs . . .
We're going to tap our noses! (tapping your knees)
We need ten of something in our song – what could we use?

At first, children will enjoy just shouting out 'No!' and correcting you. But, very soon, the older, more confident and more experienced children will be keen to tell you that they've got ten arms today or no feet or that they've forgotten to bring their face! They love to hear you say that they'd better run home and fetch them quickly or that they should bring the spare one out from their pocket or to pretend to 'catch' the spare one that you 'throw' to them and will carefully mime the 'putting on' of the correct body part because they are already deeply involved in the imaginative game.

You need to monitor this joking and pretending carefully to ensure that it only goes on for a few moments and that no child is worried or irritated by it. But sharing laughs with lots of children and the firm agreement that 'we are all ready now' is the most enthusiastic and co-operative start that you can hope for.

You need not always sit in a circle for your opening number. You could jump up when the music starts and perform it standing up or in your own spaces, or vary it from week to week.

Having warmed everybody up with a busy action song, it is a good idea to follow it immediately with a calmer one that may be more well-known but demands finer movements, such as using fingers and thumbs or hands and heads to fit the song words. This song should, ideally, be different at each session, but all of the songs could be repeated after a term or a period of ten to twelve weeks.

Figure 3 Get sessions off to an enthusiastic start using lively action songs and finger rhymes.

Young children particularly like songs and games involving hiding their hands and making them pop out again at the right time, counting on their fingers, clapping, stamping and shaking their heads. They also enjoy trying new things that they may not be able to do but would like to do, such as snapping their fingers or clapping behind their backs. As long as you make it clear that this is a more difficult thing to do and most of them are still learning, they will happily understand that they should just try their best and accept praise for effort and small advances. This is excellent preparation for later life, when they will be asked to practise and improve some skills that do not come easily to them and they will need to have a positive attitude to everybody being good at certain things and less good at others.

During a warming up period, you will be able to notice which children are close friends and whether they rely too heavily on doing things together. If you have a child who always copies another, or a pair of children who only speak to each other or who constantly giggle together instead of listening to others, you will need to decide the extent to which this may become a problem. On the day that one of the pair is feeling tired, slightly unwell or over-excited, the other will also be adversely affected, and, if one is absent from a session, the other may be unwilling or unable to join in constructively.

While accepting the importance of children's friendships, you need to encourage them to gradually work more independently. Any of us can feel happier in a situation with a familiar person present, but this needs to be seen as a valuable confidence booster that we can 'jump off from', not as an excuse to lean on someone else or to have an accomplice in being disruptive! In order for children to achieve their full potential and to feel proud of what they do, they must learn to think and behave in the way that is right for them – not for their next door neighbour or the person they sit with at school.

You might start by asking the pair of friends if another child could sit between them in the circle or if they could each have a particular child beside them. Being asked to help a younger or newer child, by demonstrating a skill in which they are already accomplished, may give them both the necessary incentive to separate and apply themselves to the task individually. However, do make sure that the younger or newer class members will appreciate the help and monitor the relationships involving over-enthusiastic children, to avoid any feelings of intimidation. During action songs, role play and the acting out of stories, offer the friends separate parts and places in lines and groups and let them know that they have been especially chosen for those parts because they are suited to their abilities.

If a group of several friends or classmates are 'sticking together' and refusing to participate fully or dominating the group too much, their behaviour may need to be dealt with quite firmly. Explaining in honest and reasonable terms why they must work as individuals within the whole class or group usually works with children from the age of 3 or 4. If they are mature enough to understand how to 'wind each other up', they are also mature enough to understand how and why they should stop!

Always give lots of praise to children as soon as they do begin to do as you have asked. Publicly applaud their individual achievements during classes and thank them privately for making any attitude or behaviour changes that were discussed and agreed with you. Children appreciate and remember specific statements of praise much more than generalities. Instead of: 'You were good in the class today, Rebecca' or 'Well done, Finlay', aim for comments such as: 'Well done, Max for sitting next to Jamie as well as Sefton in the circle today' or 'I loved the way you tapped your knees, Oscar, but you tapped your shoulders, Joseph, during the song.'

When twins, triplets or siblings attend sessions together, their particular relationships must be understood and respected, but they should also be encouraged to behave as individuals, in the same way as friends. An older child must not be expected to regularly care for a younger brother or sister to a degree that his or her own performance and enjoyment is impaired. A younger sibling may not wish to be smothered by his or her older sibling's attentions and be quite able to cope with activities without help. One twin or triplet may be more dominant or confident than the other(s) and behave in a similar way to an older sibling.

Discussion with the children's parents, carers or keyworkers is always important and will enable you to react in a manner appropriate to the children's needs and also consistent with the other adults' wishes and ideals. You will need to take on the support of the younger or less confident children yourself, or ensure that other staff members are doing so, to enable the others to work individually. You should then be able to increase confidence quickly and allow all children to take their appropriate places in the group.

It is worth remembering that there may be a larger number of minor disagreements or a greater feeling of competition between children of the same family than amongst others within the group, but these need not be taken too seriously if their parent, carer or keyworker has assured you that this is an ongoing part of their relationship and disputes are quickly forgiven and forgotten. You should merely remind the children of the usual standards of courtesy whenever necessary and offer comfort or distraction in the same way as for any children.

The overall aim during the warming up period is to bring the group together, and to encourage each child to acquire the type of attitude and focused concentration that will enable them to derive maximum benefit from each activity that follows and have fun together.

Chapter 3

Building confidence

Drama can help enormously in the building of confidence in people of any age. Learning to express yourself more clearly and practising speech and movement skills are valuable aids to developing good self-esteem. Role play situations can help with preparing for or recovering from difficult or worrying experiences, giving you the ability to 'move on' and use new skills to cope more easily in the future. Developing the imagination and flexibility to adapt to any situation quickly and do your best to join in or make things work out is an empowering life skill best learned as early as possible.

SPEAKING UP

We would all like our children to have confidence when entering new situations, to feel able to make friends and be a useful member of any group. One of the most basic skills to master is a way of introducing yourself and finding out who the other people around you are. You will also want to find out quickly what they are like and be aware of the impression you would like them to form of you. In order for children to feel comfortable with the people they interact with, you can teach them how to give their name and listen to what others are called. You can explain that this is good manners, as well as useful and interesting.

While the children are still sitting or standing in a circle, you can offer your hand to each one in turn, shaking it gently, smiling and saying: 'Hello, my name's Debbie.'

More confident and experienced children will take your hand, shake it in return and reply: 'Hello, my name's Emma.' Others will take your

Figure 4 Drama enables children to build self-confidence and learn how to interact with others.

hand and smile and nod and wait. If they are then prompted with: 'And your name is . . .?', they will reply: 'Daniel!' At this point, you can say: 'Nice to see you' or 'I'm glad you came' along with the child's name and move on to the next person in the circle.

Some children may be happy to say their name, but unwilling to take your hand, or happy to shake hands but unwilling or unable to say their name yet. Some may, at first, be unwilling to respond at all, but be pleased to be spoken to. Some children may even hide their faces in embarrassment at the first few classes or ask their parent or carer to say their name for them. The important aim here is that each child should understand that they are equally important to you and everybody is interested in who they are and keen to include them in the group.

Children learn by example and most love to copy others. If you repeat this exercise in a gentle and non-threatening way at each session, with some children responding and others watching and listening, almost all of them will gradually understand and want to join in. This is another opportunity to encourage children to wait their turn to speak, to listen to each other and to give everybody a fair chance to speak. Those who shout out, supply other children's names for them when not asked to or try to disrupt the 'listening circle' may need additional adult explanation and support to understand why this is not the best way to behave.

Practitioners or family members may choose to practise this activity with a child between drama sessions, but should avoid putting pressure on a child to 'get it right next time'!

Adults can be surprised when a child who simply didn't understand or absolutely refused to co-operate at the first two or three sessions, suddenly feels able to look at the teacher's face and give a mature reply by week four. They should celebrate the achievement of this learning objective and reward the child with praise, but avoid making too much fuss, accepting that this child is now proud of who s/he is and prepared to take a place within the group.

Once a child has been attending sessions for a year or two, you may find that he or she moves way beyond just giving a name in this situation. Children aged 4 and 5 may decide to develop the activity of their own accord, by thinking up ever longer and fancier names that they would like to have. If a child wearing a striped T-shirt tells you that his name is 'Stripey' or one with a motif on her dress announces herself as 'Butterfly', they have understood that a name is a label and, in many situations, can be their own to use as they wish. A boy who tells the circle that his name is 'Mr Cool', or a girl who announces herself under the name of 'Sparkling Fairy Tiger Lily', is demonstrating intelligence, high self-esteem and, of course, a good sense of humour!

Throughout a session, there are numerous opportunities to encourage children to speak up, sometimes as a group and sometimes individually. Ask questions after a mime session. After building up a tower of heavy bricks, ask the group:

> Who used more than five bricks?
> Whose tower is taller than their head?
> Whose tower is wobbling?
> Did anybody's tower fall down?

Ask each child individually:

> What did you build with your bricks, Kitty?
> Alexander, what did you use to stick them together?

Accept all answers as valid – sensible ones show that a child is understanding the project, but funny ones show that the child has understood that this is the world of imagination and they are in control. An imaginary

Figure 5 Some children display a wonderful sense of humour when introducing themselves to each other.

tower of bricks and cement is great, but an imaginary tower of cardboard boxes and golden syrup is just as much fun!

Choose your questions carefully according to the age, experience level and size of the group of children and be prepared to be flexible as you ask them. While the group is enjoying the game, continue to ask questions and listen to answers. If children begin to fidget or lose concentration, or if the group is large and each child's turn could take a while to come around, bring the talking to a close and move on to the next activity, ensuring that each child has had at least one opportunity to speak.

PERFORMANCE SKILLS

It is very valuable for children to experience standing and working 'onstage'. So many adults wish that they could have had the opportunity to perform in some way after leaving school, or that they could join an amateur theatre company or take part in a concert or exhibition, but feel too overcome with embarrassment or lack confidence in their own abilities, and do not do it.

Not all children enjoy the 'school play' each year or the 'class assemblies' before the whole school, but most do. If children are used to standing up before others regularly from a very young age and speaking out, singing, dancing or performing in any other way, they will be able to use these skills in any situation they encounter later and never have to miss an opportunity that they wish they could have taken.

In a school or nursery setting, you may be lucky enough to have a stage or stage blocks that can be easily assembled for use in at least some of your drama sessions. This may also apply to a hired hall for private classes. If not, try to make a special area which you can call 'our stage', using gym mats, rugs or blankets, a brick surround or lines chalked on the floor. Adults should take extra care to explain to and remind children of the dangers of standing too close to the edges of a raised stage and be extra vigilant in supervision while children are onstage or climbing up or down.

Children can be encouraged to stand in a line or a group onstage and shout out phrases to any adults or baby siblings forming their audience or to a picture on the back wall. This ensures that they have no fear of speaking out in a room or hall when they know that they have something valid to say. If this fear never develops, it will not crop up in later life. Telling them that important and special people stand onstage and that it makes other people want to listen to you, as well as joining them and showing your excitement and pleasure to be on a stage, help to develop the attitude you are aiming for.

Suitable phrases to say onstage might be:

Hello everybody!
Welcome to our drama class!
Today is Monday!
Today we've been thinking about jungle animals!

Encourage the children to speak and enunciate clearly and project their voices, rather than shouting as loudly as they can until the sounds and words are lost. Praise those who try particularly hard, whether they are achieving the objective for the first time or reliably improving at each session. Ensure that every child knows what is to be said before you begin and is ready to focus and concentrate. Count them in with 'one, two, three' or 'ready and go', or anything similar, and they will be beginning to learn about timing and working as a member of a team without even realising it.

As soon as enough children are ready for the experience, ask them to speak out individually onstage, taking their cue from whoever is next to them in the line. Explain carefully what they should try to say and expect that each child will be listened to by the others. Ask an adult to stand beside a child who tries to call out or disrupt others' listening, to model and encourage correct responses and discourage others from copying the unwanted behaviour. If a child is unhappy or unable to participate or listen onstage, ask an adult to take the child into the 'audience' to watch the others and rejoin the group for the next activity.

This is another confidence building activity that children can learn gradually. It is extremely rewarding to see a young child who cried when taken onstage for the first time, or one with delayed speech who was unable to say anything at early classes, proudly shouting out their name, age and favourite colour to an audience!

Figure 6 It is rewarding to watch each child develop the confidence to stand and speak clearly onstage.

Building on the 'introducing yourself' work covered earlier in the session, children can be asked to say their name along with their age or where they live, or to contribute an imaginative idea of their own. Early sessions could involve phrases such as:

My name is Martha and I'm three.
My name is Luke and I live in Cambridge.

Later sessions could move on to:

My name is Alex and I like blue and red.
My name is Hannah and I like pink crocodiles.

Sessions for experienced children could lead to more detail in speech and acting skills:

My name is Pip and if I was in the jungle I would like to be an elephant!
(accompanied by a demonstration of an elephant)

My name is Sleeping Beauty and my favourite character in my story is the prince who cuts down the trees to come and give me a kiss and wake me up!
(accompanied by a demonstration of a princess sleeping and/or a prince on his horse cutting through a forest)

Some children will always think up their own idea, while some may usually copy the most popular idea or that of whoever is next to them. Be aware that sometimes a child standing further down the line will have thought up the same idea independently and will not change it just because somebody else has thought of it too, while others are only gradually understanding what to do, and coping with their position in the line is enough of a new learning experience for the moment. Accept and praise all contributions, but take particular notice of the child who contributes an original idea which is especially amusing or apt for the situation.

If a child would like to tell you their idea, but is not prepared to say it loudly enough for others to hear, come down to their level and accept the contribution in as enthusiastic a manner as all the others, repeating it aloud for the group to share. It is a good idea to clap each child when they finish speaking and encourage your 'audience' to do so too. This helps them to remember why they are speaking out and makes it clear to the next child that it is definitely their turn now.

After the speech activities, and any singing, dancing or acting that you choose to carry out onstage, ask the children to take a bow before they carefully come offstage. At first, or when time is short, they can all bow together as a group. Individual bows may be taken once children understand the idea of taking cues from each other and are happy to take their turn alone. This is an opportunity for more applause from you and your 'audience'. Some children may ask if they may curtsey instead and all children should be permitted to choose. It does not matter, of course, which of the children prefer to bow or curtsey. No distinctions should be made between boys and girls at this age and each child may choose to try out either or both, selecting the same option or a different one at each class.

Some children will answer any question put to the group and challenge any 'deliberate mistake', so long as nobody, especially the teacher, looks at them directly and asks them by name. Others will only speak up when particularly asked, if they are sure that the other children will wait and listen to them.

Some children are much more confident when seated beside their friend or within a group of children that they know well. Others prefer to join a private class and find their own place before assessing the potential for friendships. Sometimes a child will be less confident because their keyworker is absent or they are attending a class with their mother instead of their nanny, or more confident because today granny has come along to watch the class. Some children are naturally quieter or noisier than others most of the time. Each child will gradually decrease their dependence on the support or the presence of their parent or carer as their confidence increases. If they receive careful and appropriate encouragement, they will be able to do this at the pace that is right for them.

The overall aim is for each and every child, whatever their age, level of experience or ability or degree of special need, to gradually increase their confidence in themselves, their abilities and their knowledge that they are a worthwhile person. Then they may achieve whatever they wish to achieve, in the way that they feel is right for them, without the frustration of feeling that they 'can't do it'. This is an attitude that will help them throughout their life.

Chapter 4

Encouraging social interaction

Drama is essentially a social activity. Although some adult performers may occasionally sing, act a play or a monologue or tell jokes alone, even they are supported by an orchestra, a backstage crew or a team behind the cameras. They may also need a prompter, a costume designer, a make-up artist or someone to keep track of all their props for them. Most performers are team players and must make good relationships with those with whom they work. This may mean getting to know a large number of people very quickly and then saying goodbye to them again and joining a completely new team, knowing that some of these people may work together on another project in the future, while others may never meet again. Luckily, getting to know people quickly is easy when you are acting and performing with them. Making up a story, pretending to be a character or an animal, taking part in a dance or song together and sharing laughter are friendly things to do.

LETTING FRIENDSHIPS DEVELOP

It is important to encourage social interaction between young children from the beginning, without forcing them to make relationships that they are not yet ready for. Asking everybody to sit together in a circle or a group is enough to encourage some children to choose friends to sit next to and giggle with. Others will neither need nor want this at first. Allowing children to sit beside or even on the laps of their familiar carers can give them the confidence to join in with a circle activity. But you should always ask them to sit within the circle and not behind it or some distance away, emphasising the social situation of friends coming together to share a drama class.

Gradually encourage children to sit closer to each other and to choose their own places in the circle, sensitively ensuring that no particular children are the ones always chosen or never chosen as the 'friends' that others wish to sit next to. As unobtrusively as possible, take to sit beside you the children who have the most need to do so or who would derive the greatest benefit from doing so, but, as far as possible, ensure that it is not the same children who do this at each class.

Gradually decrease the amount of direction that you offer to the group of children at certain times, as you feel that they are gaining in social confidence. Allow short breaks for children to chat and laugh with each other, or just to exchange friendly looks and smiles. Don't talk all the time! Take a few moments to change a tape, find a book or press a button on a CD player if you sense that some children would like to speak to each other and others would like to relax for a couple of minutes before concentrating on another new dramatic task.

There may be times when children would like to tell you about something important to them. This may be a happy or a traumatic event in their lives, or just something that they presently find very interesting. Try to make available various short timeslots during which this kind of talking could be appropriate. If they only want to talk to you, it may need to be before or after the session. But, if it is something that they would like to share with the whole group, everybody might enjoy listening during a short break after each child has been introduced, or after a busy action song, or just before a story is read.

It is important to encourage all children to understand that they should want to listen to their peers and take an interest in what they have to say and that they should feel able to share their own observations and events with the group and expect that others will listen to them in return.

If a recent event or experience has affected several or all of the children in the group, they may want to tell you about it. Encourage them to share the telling of a story, asking questions and prompting as necessary to display the correct level of interest, but not altering or directing the way the story is told. Gently remind more confident children that others would like to speak too and ask them to wait for a few seconds from time to time. Invite quieter or more timid children to volunteer their opinions too and ask others to listen to them. Taking part in a group conversation is a valuable skill to learn, and one which some children will find easier than others. The aim is to develop confidence in knowing when would be an appropriate moment to speak or to listen and expecting that others will observe the same standards. Once this confidence is established, taking part in conversations becomes enjoyable.

Try to think of events in your own life that the children may be able to relate to and find interesting and model this kind of general conversation for them to imitate. They may enjoy hearing about the things your own children do and say, or used to do and say when they were younger, about your pets, holidays you have taken, places you have visited, new things you have bought or learned, minor things that went wrong for you or events you are looking forward to. They need to understand that adults also inhabit a less than perfect world and have to cope with life and other people every day, have the same range of feelings and emotions as when they were younger, but have merely learned more self-control and do not always make their feelings so obvious.

Show children that you can feel wonder and amazement, joy, sadness, anger and understanding and encourage them to do the same, expressing themselves both verbally and non-verbally but with appreciation of others' needs and feelings. This is a valuable learning experience in social interaction and will help to cement a friendship between you to enable you to work together productively.

You will need to become aware very quickly of which children achieve more and are less disruptive to the group if they are directed towards activities separately. It may be appropriate to seat them away from each other in any circle or group, but avoid always taking them to sit beside you or paying them extra attention that could be interpreted as rewards by the other children, or the unwanted behaviours may be copied! A new or timid child may be wary or afraid of interacting with more confident or boisterous children at first and will make greater progress if placed beside slightly quieter and calmer class members. Getting to know the abilities and personalities of every member of the group is crucial.

IN A NURSERY OR SCHOOL SETTING

Children's friendships may already be well developed or forming rapidly and staff in the setting will usually be monitoring and assisting this each day. Drama sessions may offer extension activities that further develop children's ability to relate to each other and work together. Be guided by staff observations as to which children may achieve more or less if they work together or separately, and discuss together, out of the children's hearing, any relationships that you would like to encourage. In this way, all the adults in the setting may work consistently for the benefit of all the children.

IN PRIVATE CLASSES

Some children may attend a class with friends and others may know nobody when they first join the group. Encourage new friendships to form whenever you see the opportunity for them, but be aware of how constructive the relationships may eventually be. Some parents and carers bring their children to classes because they are hoping that the children may make some new friends, but others are very busy people and are only looking for their children to enjoy the drama experience.

There is no point in trying to encourage a friendship between children outside sessions if you know that it would be doomed to failure. For example: one family may keep three dogs while the other is allergic to pet hair; one family may smoke at home while the other is severely asthmatic; one family may live in the city and the other in a rural village but neither has access to a car on most days of the week; one child's older brother or sister may have bullied the other child's sibling at school and involved the families in bitter recriminations in the past; one family may have just left a childcare situation due to dissatisfaction, while the other family thinks it is the best place they have ever seen. The list is endless and you cannot be expected to know of all possible scenarios, but you should avoid assuming that, just because children appear to like each other while participating in a class, they could be best friends outside it. Always err on the side of caution. It is possible to explain to children that it is fun to have special friends that you only see at drama sessions and would not otherwise have met at all.

If adults are staying to participate in or watch the class, they will see relationships for themselves and usually monitor the situation in the way that they wish to. If they are leaving their child with you, they may like to be told which members of the group the child seems to particularly like, or they may want to ask you about those their child mentions between classes. Parents and carers have a right to know about the people that their children associate with, but you must be professional and not give out confidential information or details on any child or family. If you are asked a question that you are unsure whether to answer, or a parent requests the contact details of another, you must first ask the other family how they feel about it or introduce them to each other and let them make their own decisions.

GAMES AND ACTIVITIES

There are many opportunities for children to interact socially during action songs, dancing and listening games. Pairs and small groups can be formed by the leader, by all the adults or by the children themselves. Begin with simple examples and progress along with the children at the pace set naturally by them.

ACTIONS TO ENCOURAGE SOCIAL INTERACTION

These activities can be introduced as mimes or as parts of acted stories or action songs and will be adult-led:

- Rowing an imaginary boat.
- Throwing and catching an imaginary ball.
- Riding on an imaginary seesaw.
- Taking turns to describe what you built or found, saw or chose.
- Playing ring games.

These activities can be suggested by the adult, but then led by the children.

- Dancing freely to music with a partner or in a ring of three or four children.
- Dancing with a partner and helping each other to freeze or sit down when the music stops.
- Searching or digging for imaginary items of treasure and bringing them back to share with the group at random.
- Creating an imaginary sandcastle or brick tower as a whole group or within smaller groups, finding items to use and helping it to balance.

Figure 7 New friendships can develop as children act and dance together.

Figure 8 Children learn to work together as they share characters and movements.

DEGREES OF INTERACTION

Some people will always be happy to follow the crowd, while others will always prefer to be different. Both of these types of people, and every combination of person between the two extremes, can be accepted for who they are. Children need to learn to judge when one particular type of behaviour would be more appropriate than another, mostly through adults setting good examples and offering opportunities for them to experience social situations. While those who think for themselves, develop ideas and embrace imagination are important to our world, we all need to understand when it is necessary to conform to an accepted social standard and learn to do this as we grow up. (While a toddler might be forgiven for throwing a toy across a doctors' waiting room or shouting in a library, an older child would be frowned upon by others sharing the facility and an adult would be asked to leave!)

Somewhere between the age of 3 and the age of 6, most children learn how to wait their turn for an adult's attention, how to listen to their friends as well as talk to them, how to stand quietly in a queue, how to ask politely for what they would like and to say thank you when they receive it and to accept that they cannot always have exactly what they want immediately – sometimes they must wait for it and sometimes they cannot have it at all!

These are all important skills that will enable them to get on in the world, because others will like them, listen and talk to them and invite them to join in with their games and activities. The child who shouts above all his classmates at every discussion time, can't stand or sit still when others are doing so, never listens to instructions or watches examples and expects others to make allowances but never does so in return, will be the one in trouble at school and in clubs, and also in danger of being excluded from friendships, birthday parties, outings and treats because other children and parents feel uncomfortable.

A child should be praised for thinking up or using original ideas that fit within a context, but one who copies those around is also learning to conform socially. The child who seems completely unaware of what others are doing and unable to copy or adapt the activity to join in with it is the one who should give cause for concern. A lack of any kind of social interaction coupled with a lack of any desire for it could make a practitioner suspect that a child has a degree of disability or special need. The child who does not respond, listen or speak may have a hearing loss, while the one who makes a lot of noise but refuses to sit down near to any other person or to move on to a different activity may have a communication difficulty such as autism.

TACTILE EXPERIENCES

Through drama, children can come to know their own bodies and what they can do with them very well. They may work on action songs that involve pointing to or moving various parts of the body and learn to walk, run, jump, hop, skip, tiptoe, 'skate', take giant steps or tiny ones, dance, creep, crawl, roll, stop and freeze. They will become more confident that they can use their own bodies to interact with others in the group, both by touching each other and by avoiding collisions when dancing or moving around.

It is a good idea to offer a group song at the end of a session which involves everybody holding hands in a circle. If the same song is used at each class, the children will get used to the actions and be prepared to hold hands at the appropriate time. They will probably not be ready to do this at the beginning of a class, but may do it easily by the middle of the session if a well-known ring game is introduced. Reinforcing it at the end allows children to go away from the session with the warm feeling that they have been working with friends, and makes them more eager to return.

If a child is not yet ready to hold hands with other children, you could try temporarily placing an adult at one or both sides of the child, or inviting the child to move forward and sit within the circle while others hold hands around (not backwards, where they would feel excluded by the circle of hands), or sitting the child on your lap or between your legs while you hold the hands of those beside you. Offer every child the same chance to join hands at each session and offer praise but make no fuss as each one finally develops the courage to participate. Don't have set places for children within the circle, but ask them all to come and join in by sitting or standing in any space available, so that they are beside different friends each time.

Your ultimate aim is for every child to be happy to take the hands of the children on either side, whoever they are. (This is a skill and attitude that they may go on to be glad to have practised when they were younger, as it may be required in primary and secondary school and any adult joining an amateur theatre group or taking part in a team building workshop will need it!)

Some people naturally touch and hug others often, while some never get that close to anyone outside their immediate family. Some children will come from families who pick them up and cuddle them a lot, while some will maintain their relationships much more through talking or doing things together. Explain to the group that holding hands or dancing together is just something that is fun to do and only lasts as long as the song or activity.

GETTING IN AND GETTING OUT

Be at your most persuasive and ask all children to join in with the first and last activities, because the entering and leaving of any social situation are the hardest parts. They need to begin to learn and develop these skills as early as possible, to allow them plenty of time to practise them.

Most people agree that they can do what they thought of as 'scary' things once they get started, or as soon as they get going, or when they are used to them. The only problem then is how and when to stop without missing the best part, offending somebody or boring them!

Chapter 5

Mime and expression

Very young children are naturally very expressive and will readily display their emotions for all to see, particularly when they are excited, displeased or upset! They can have a lot of fun learning to express themselves without sound or speech in a variety of games and activities. This will also help them gradually to learn to develop self-control in certain situations, to communicate with others of all ages and from all walks of life and to understand and empathise with other people's feelings.

Children are learning vocabulary all the time at this age and they love new words of all kinds. Never be afraid to use the correct words for the activities you are sharing with young children. They will not see one word as being more complicated or hard to remember than another, but will respond constructively to any words that are repeated frequently and used in a meaningful context. (But their parents and carers are likely to be impressed by their confident use of correct stage terminology and respond with praise and enthusiasm!)

At the appropriate time during each session, say to them that you are now going to work on some special acting without any talking or sounds and that this is called . . . miming! Within two or three weeks, most of them will finish the sentence for you, as well as recognising mime situations in other parts of their lives and telling all their other family members and carers about mime. They will also come to understand that acting means one thing standing for another, just as it does in their role play, and begin to appreciate the meanings of words such as symbolic, action, sequence and expression.

GAMES TO PLAY TO ENCOURAGE EXPRESSIVE MIME

Begin with a simple game of 'making faces'. The youngest children will prefer to sit in a circle, so that they are all facing each other. Slightly older ones may enjoy sitting or standing in two lines, so that they are facing a partner, but encourage them to look at the faces of all those near to them, not just one other child. Ask the children to show you a face and model it for them, making sure that they can all see you clearly and understand that this is acting and pretending, and should be exaggerated.

A range of expressions for faces alone can be taught, such as:

happy, sad, worried, frightened, tired, surprised, thinking, excited – and (the children's favourite) – cross!

Encourage the use of arms and hands to enhance expressions if children are ready:

- hands on hips or arms folded can emphasise being cross:
- hands to mouth can add to a worried or frightened look;
- rubbing eyes or covering a yawn goes well with a tired face;
- hands raised look surprised;
- a finger on a chin indicates thinking;
- clenched fists close to the body enhance an excited expression.

Younger children will enjoy making the same faces over and over again until they feel very sure of what each expression means and how it makes them feel. But, for your own sake and the sake of the other adults present, it is sensible to vary the order in which they are made.

Have a selection of ten or twelve different ones prepared and work on a different combination of four, six or eight of them at each session. This allows enough repetition for the children, without the adults becoming too bored to participate enthusiastically! Gradually ask the children to change their expressions more and more quickly as they become more confident and proficient at remembering them.

Once a range of expressions have been introduced, discussed and practised and the children are familiar with them, play games such as:

Make the face I call out.

Guess which face I'm making and call out its name.

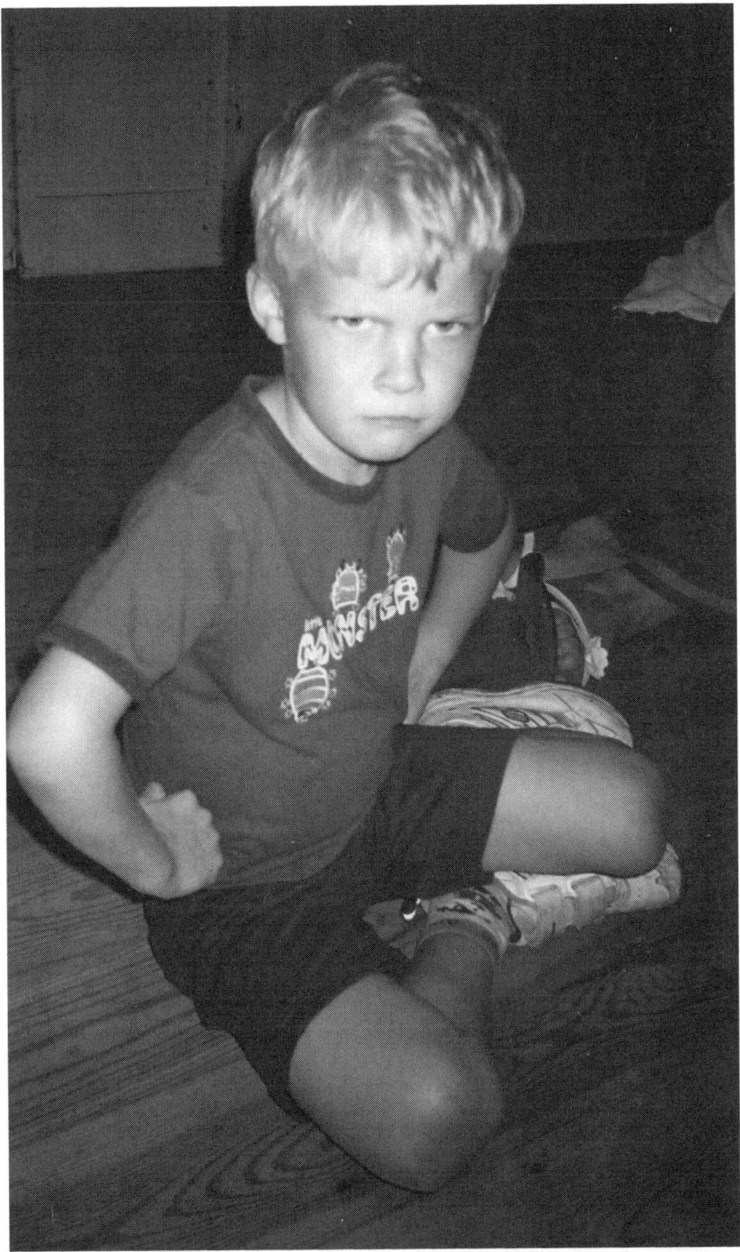

Figure 9 Children quickly learn to mime expressions – 'cross' being a favourite choice!

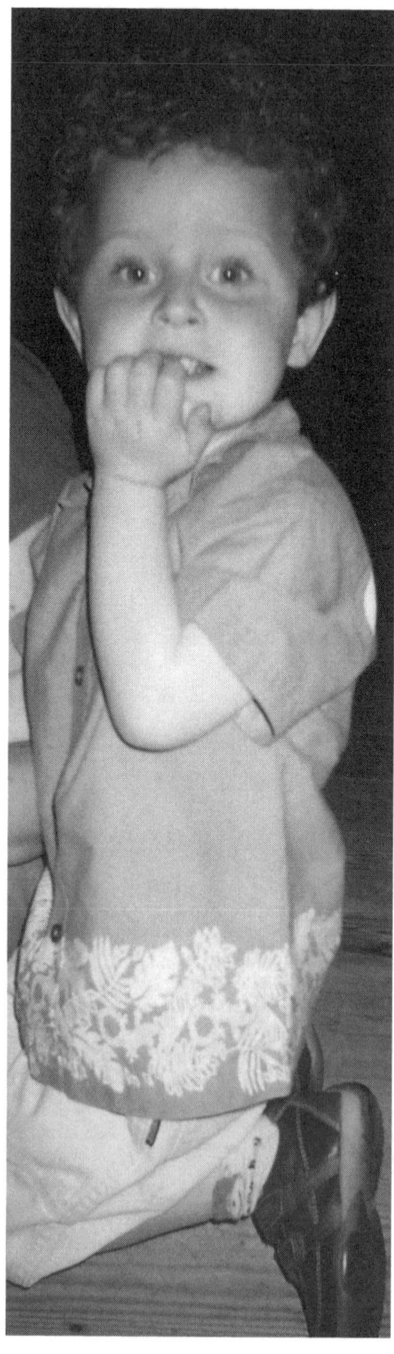

Figure 10 'Worried' is a dramatic expression that children enjoy using when acting out stories.

Copy the face I make and change it when I do.
Take turns to show us all your favourite expression.
Show your favourite expression to the person sitting next to you.

Some children will become confident enough to enjoy showing an expression to the whole group or making a face for the whole group to guess. Others will not be ready to do this until after they leave the foundation stage. If a few within the group are ready to move on to this level of learning, they should be encouraged to do so, but no very young child should be expected to 'take the lead' in this way unless they are happy to. It can be difficult to be sure in some cases, as children of this age will not reliably put up their hands or form a group if they wish to participate, or move aside if they don't! Some children find it hard to understand exactly what is being asked in a whole group situation.

But a child can become upset or have their confidence lowered if they are overlooked because a well-meaning adult thought that they did not want to join in, when, in fact, they just did not want to jump up and down and shout out that they wanted to take a turn. It is best to offer each individual child the opportunity to do it and accept their response sensitively and without fuss whether they agree or refuse, repeating the offer at regular intervals, such as every two or three weeks.

Some children will agree to any new experience and happily try their best, not worrying about making any mistakes, as long as they feel secure and supported within the learning situation. Some will refuse a couple of times, but watch how others do it until they are absolutely sure of what is being suggested and then eagerly request their turn. Others will refuse for a term or longer, but still enjoy and learn from watching how other children approach the task in their various ways. Recognising which type of person they are within a group situation and feeling comfortable with this is another important learning experience for a child. This can only come through practical experiences, where the support of sensitive and experienced practitioners can ensure that each child feels positive about him or herself, whatever their abilities and talents.

It is important that you take care to praise one child for their abilities in expression and mime, another for their talent in dance and movement and another for their original ideas in speechwork, making it clear that we are all differently able but all good at something and each skill is equally valuable. The most useful praise is that which recognises a child's improvement in a skill they were struggling with or lacked confidence in, however slight the improvement, and any effort a child is making to overcome a difficulty or increase a proficiency.

USING THE WHOLE BODY FOR MIME AND EXPRESSION

Once they are used to making expressions with their faces, children will naturally start to enhance them with their arms and upper bodies and should be encouraged to do so. If you ask them to stand up and use their legs too, their mimes will become even more sophisticated. Try mimes such as:

seeing a friend and waving hello;
feeling sad at having to say goodbye;
asking your friend to come here;
lifting a heavy box;
pushing a heavy wheelbarrow;
flying a kite;
searching through a drawer or cupboard;
knocking at a door;
opening a door;
splashing in a puddle;
climbing a mountain;
running down a slope;
digging a hole;
making and decorating a sandcastle;
playing on a slide and a seesaw;
putting on a coat, hat, scarf and gloves;
making a snowman;
rolling in a pile of leaves.

MOVING ON TO MIMING SEQUENCES, CHARACTERS AND STORIES

Children can easily be encouraged to move on to using their whole bodies for mime. Begin by making up a simple story sequence and encourage children to participate in portraying the story in mime, by asking questions and demonstrating actions of your own alongside them. A simple example could be:

What might I look like if I was a very old person?
And how might I walk?
How might I move if I was feeling very tired and thirsty?
How do you think I would feel if the rain fell on me?
What might I need to use?
How would I hold it?
What would happen if the wind blew strongly?
And then how would I feel if the sun came out?
How would I feel when I got home at last?
What would I do first when I got there?

Simple sequences that children can learn to perform from memory are:

- climbing stairs, putting on pyjamas, cleaning teeth, finding teddy and going to bed;
- digging a hole, planting seeds, watering seeds, sitting in sun, seeing seeds grow into flowers;
- fetching bricks in wheelbarrow, mixing cement, building wall or tower;
- putting on outdoor clothes; making footprints in snow, making snowman;
- catching train to seaside, digging sandcastle, swimming in sea, taking train home again;
- meeting friend, playing on swing, slide, seesaw and roundabout, saying goodbye.

You will need to explain to the children frequently that there are no right and wrong ways to mime a word or action. If another person understands what you mean, your mime is successful (and even if they don't, it may still be entertaining!).

It may be helpful and constructive for a group working together to agree on certain basic mimes to indicate frequently used words and actions, or it may be more appropriate for each individual to interpret them in their own way. Encourage all members of the group to be as inventive as they like and to share and discuss new ideas with others.

If you have any children or adults with special needs or a degree of hearing loss within the group, or children who are not yet proficient in the language the lesson is conducted in, mime will be an area in which they can always participate on an equal level with everybody else.

If any type of sign language is known or used by any member of the group, it can be incorporated into mime activities. It is an excellent idea for any practitioner intending to teach or use drama with young children to learn basic skills in one or more sign languages and be prepared to use them.

Makaton is particularly appropriate for young children and easy to learn and use. Many of the signs for basic and frequently used words are almost identical to the ones a person would probably make up if asked to mime them, but there are subtle differences which help to avoid confusion between similar words, such as the greetings 'hello' and 'goodbye'. It is designed to be used alongside speech, rather than to replace it completely, and so may well be a breakthrough in helping those still learning the language to feel more confident in making themselves understood in other areas as well as in mime activities.

Some songs lend themselves well to mime. Most nursery rhymes can be acted out in mime, but many of them require lots of different actions following each other very quickly, so the simplest songs to sing are not always the simplest for use in mime. Try to begin with very simple action songs and move on to miming characters and stories as the group grows in experience, confidence and proficiency.

Look out for children's songs which describe a particular action or project and offer lots of opportunities for repetition, such as songs about:

building a house or a tower;
digging the garden or field and planting seeds;
sleeping and waking;
working with various tools;
driving or being various vehicles;
moving as various animals;
jumping, stamping, hopping, tiptoeing, etc.

It is a simple step from these sequences and songs to move on to acting out simple stories involving characters that the children know and like. Read or tell a story, using a book, poster or pictures and encourage much discussion and group participation. Then, challenge the children to re-tell the story in mime. Work alongside them, performing appropriate actions and mimes and prompting them with cues if necessary, to ensure that they can move from the beginning of the story to the end without omitting a part that they would like to include.

Figure 11
Children think deeply about new characters and stories that are introduced to them.

Always praise the group as a whole at the end of this project, telling them what a good story they made together. This is an excellent way of encouraging teamwork and making each child feel that they are an important member of the group.

The children will love it if you can supply appropriate character toys and speak to them, letting them whisper into your ear how clever they thought all the children were at acting and how pleased they are to have come, then bow and wave to the children before returning to their bag or box to have a sleep! Visual aids of this kind can encourage the most timid and the most uncooperative children to participate and ensure that all children remember the story and activity well enough to recount it to other family members or carers later.

When children spontaneously talk about an activity and obviously remember it with enjoyment, other adults will be able to appreciate its value and the learning experience will be enhanced for everybody who is involved in any way.

Chapter 6

Movement and dance

During the foundation stage, children spend a great deal of their time learning to control their own bodies and exploring what they can do with them. It is important that they are given enough time and opportunities to work and play with their whole bodies and to gradually develop basic gross and fine motor skills and the confidence to use them. Young children learn through doing things and they learn more quickly if they enjoy what they are doing.

As well as through their own play, most children enjoy developing and reinforcing their movement skills alongside others in nurseries, pre-schools and schools and in private classes for drama, dance, sport or gymnastics, under the leadership and supervision of qualified practitioners.

BASIC MOVEMENT SKILLS FOR USE IN DRAMA

In order to act and portray characters and situations happily, children need to feel confident that they can make their own bodies show what they are thinking. In early sessions with any group, you must find out what stage each child has reached in the development of motor skills and offer them all opportunities to reinforce these and move on at an appropriate level. Basic skills to check include:

> walking; running; jumping; hopping; skipping; stamping; galloping; tiptoeing; skating; spinning; climbing; balancing; dancing.

Very young children may not yet be able to hop or skip proficiently, but they can learn what the movements look and feel like by holding onto an

Figure 12 Children learn through drama that they can make their bodies show what they are thinking.

adult or a wall for balance and trying to copy others who are willing to demonstrate. They need to gradually come to understand the difference between galloping, which involves leading with the same leg throughout the movement, and skipping, which involves changing the leading leg with each step.

A skating movement means sliding feet across the floor and taking care with balance. A climbing movement means lifting legs and feet high with arms held up, as though on a ladder or mountain. Balancing can mean standing on one leg, walking along a string, painted or imaginary line on the floor or assuming various dance or gymnastic positions. Dancing simply means moving to music in a rhythmic and enjoyable manner.

These movements may be practised on their own, to suitable pieces of music or within action songs and rhymes. Children need to spend lots of time moving around in large spaces, and, if they are offered specific opportunities to learn and practise movements under the guidance of practitioners, they will naturally use them in their play at other times. Feeling that they are able to control their own bodies well enough to move around amongst others safely and co-operatively, avoiding accidents and confusions, is essential for children's growing confidence and self-esteem. And children who are proficient at basic movement skills are also likely to be confident and accomplished when using play equipment such as climbing frames and tricycles – another health and safety bonus!

FREQUENT AND REGULAR MOVEMENT OPPORTUNITIES

If possible, organise a regular time during each day or week to practise movements. Within a nursery or pre-school, this might be just before circle or snack time or after story time, every day or on two or three days a week. If children attend the setting on a sessional basis, rather than full- or half-time, ensure that each child will have a chance to participate at least once a week. In a reception class, children will have designated times for PE lessons, but they should also have access to an outdoor space not only at playtimes, which can be used for extra movement activities on the other days of the week. In wet and wintry weather, it may be possible to ask for extra time in the hall, or to push the furniture back and turn the classroom into a drama studio!

If children attend private classes once a week, follow a format which devotes particular time to the developing of new movement skills at a

Figure 13 Moving to music develops co-ordination skills.

regular point in the class. It usually works well to do this fairly early in the session, once the children are settled but before any of them get tired. For example, you could start with a warm-up song, then welcome everybody and offer a mime or acting activity to bring the group together. After this, the children will be ready and eager to use their whole bodies to move around and action songs, dances and working on a mixture of well-known and new gross motor skills will be popular. Adjust the length of this activity for a few weeks until you have decided at which point most children are happily tiring and ready to do something else and then follow it with a quieter activity, such as speaking a rhyme or listening to and acting out a story.

SAFETY AND CARE

Before letting children loose to set off around the room at random, do establish some safety rules and give some warnings about taking reasonable care. Demonstrate sensible behaviour and silly behaviour, so that even the youngest or least verbal child can understand the possible consequences of losing control. During quick movements, such as running or galloping, all children should be travelling in the same direction around the room and looking out for others all the time, to avoid collisions. During slow movements, such as tiptoeing or stamping, children may enjoy weaving around each other and this will help to make them more aware of the amount of space they need for their body to pass safely among a crowd of others. We all need to have this spatial awareness before we can venture out into the streets without an adult's hand or a pushchair!

Inevitably, with this age group, there are bound to be a few bumps and bruises occasionally. Young children do trip over their own feet and fall for no apparent reason when they are running or dancing. They will sometimes bump into each other, because they cannot yet be fully aware of their own movements and those of everybody else around them at the same time (if they could, they would not need these opportunities for movement within the foundation stage). They are gradually learning and developing greater self-control and will stop doing this once they have absorbed this stage of learning and moved on. As long as only minor accidents occur, children may be easily comforted with a tissue and a cuddle and will usually be eager to join in again within a few minutes.

It is important to ensure that the cleared space is large enough for the group of moving children, that the floor surface is safe and not too hard and that there is no furniture sticking out that could be dangerous to small heads or eyes.

IN PRIVATE CLASSES

Children (and parents and carers) in private classes need to be discouraged from bringing food and drinks and toys into the working space before and during the sessions, as these can become hazardous for all the children. A wet floor is slippery and so are biscuit crumbs or raisins scattered by a baby sibling. A soft teddy or a plastic truck left on the floor can trip a child dancing by. Children can be fascinated by toys belonging to others and this can cause problems when a child is understandably reluctant to share a special item or a group is distracted by the charms of the toy.

If possible, provide an adjoining room or separate space for babies to eat and play, or tactfully ask and remind parents and carers to keep them to the sides of the room or to put them into pushchairs to eat and play. Obviously, no child should ever be allowed to participate in a class holding food or a drink, or with a dummy in a mouth. You may choose to allow children to hold their soft toys within a seated circle for speechwork or an action song, or to dance with them during a listening skills game such as Musical Statues, if you feel that they help the shyer children to speak up or join in. But at all other times it is best to have a special place for any toys from home to sit and watch the class and to be prepared to admire them and discuss them with children only before and after sessions.

IN SCHOOLS AND NURSERIES

Always observe the correct ratio of adults to children of the age group you are working with, with extras if they are available. Two-year-olds and children with special needs may require an adult each, or one per two children. Ideally a group should not consist of more than fifteen to sixteen children working on drama at a time, except in a school reception class where there is enough space and the children are working with the classmates and adults that they are used to on a daily basis.

The leader of a nursery or pre-school class or group should always be supernumery, to avoid the session grinding to a halt because of one child becoming hurt or upset or needing to go to the toilet. This may not be possible in a school reception class, as the class teacher will always be included in the ratio, but these children may go to the toilet alone, the teaching assistant will be used to dealing with all minor upsets and there are always other adults not far away who can be called upon to assist in any emergency.

ENCOURAGING SAFE BEHAVIOUR

Children who find it hard to move safely amongst a group or who become very excited and unable to maintain self-control can be encouraged to stand still and watch with a practitioner or parent for a few minutes and talk about how other children are managing to avoid each other and look where they are going, then to gradually join in while holding the adult's hand, until they feel able to try again alone. This process of asking a child to come out temporarily can be repeated whenever a child's behaviour becomes potentially hazardous to him/herself or others. It should be seen as a part of the learning experience and not as a punishment.

A child who does continue to deliberately push or bump into others or scream and run wildly, even after repeated requests and warnings, may need to be temporarily removed from the situation. This child may need one-to-one adult assistance to learn to join in safely with the activity on future occasions and lots of praise each time he/she makes a movement in an acceptable manner.

Ring games can be an excellent way of teaching some movements to a whole group and making everybody feel involved. Children and parents usually enjoy them and they can be a great way to cheer everybody up on a dull day; you will feel spirits rise as a 'party mood' takes over. But these can be limiting, can place an emphasis on 'getting it right' and do not allow for much free expression. So, it is best to keep a few favourite games for the beginning and end of sessions (and parties) and to use them sparingly at other times.

Do not be afraid to let the children go! Some sessions held in small rooms by inexperienced practitioners can involve children (and sometimes their parents and carers too) in copying a succession of words, actions and movements without ever moving out of a circle, for more than half an hour. This is not an ideal way for young children to learn. Children need to be able to set off on their own path around the room and try out their own ideas. The practitioner leading the session needs to be able to watch each child individually and see that what they are doing is valuable, praising those developing greater skills, encouraging those trying something new and calming those becoming more excited than constructive.

This requires experience and confidence. If you are sure that you know how your group of children is likely to react and behave and you believe that they will come back together when you ask them to and offer the next activity, you will be able to facilitate their real learning experiences.

CHANGING THE FORMATION

While children thrive on repetition and familiar experiences, they are always willing to embrace new challenges and try out new activities, if they feel secure and supported within the situation and the setting. Young children can concentrate for extended periods of time if they are interested in what they are doing and enjoying exploring an activity, but their attention span can be brief and, if they become bored, they will be unable to learn or develop skills or maintain the type and level of behaviour that allows the group to work together.

It is important to change the activity frequently. Aim to offer a new project in an inviting manner at least every ten minutes in a drama class. Experienced children may manage to stay engaged for up to fifteen minutes at a time by the last year of the foundation stage, but they will appreciate the chance to participate in shorter activities between the longer ones. Ensure that quieter work, such as speaking a rhyme or miming a sequence, alternates with noisier work, such as dancing, actions and movement.

Simply changing the activity, however, is not enough. If the children are asked to sit, stand or move always within a circle or in their own spaces on a carpet, or in a line facing the teacher, they will not feel the differences within their bodies and come to each new activity refreshed and happy to start again. Begin and end with a circle, to reinforce the idea of friendship and teamwork, and aid social skills and the ability to conform to a group when required. But ask the children to move from the circle into a line, then into their own spaces all over the room, then into two lines facing each other, then into a marching line with one behind another, then into a group to share a story and act it out.

Avoid telling them exactly where to sit and stand during some projects, but, instead, show them how you are using the space available and encourage them to follow you and develop their own ideas as they work.

Praise children for the creative use of space, such as crawling low along the floor or reaching high into the air when acting out a creature or character. Thank them when they use space sensibly for the good of those around them, such as making room for another child to join in, going without fuss to the most obvious space left within a line or circle, or checking carefully for room before making a large or fast movement, such as running or galloping. If children learn from a young age how to assess the space in any situation and move into and out of it constructively without upsetting or distracting others, they will be developing a very valuable skill that will contribute to their abilities, their confidence and their self-esteem throughout their lives.

PROMOTING UNDERSTANDING

Whatever a child's age or level of ability, your first aim is to teach them the words we use to describe various types of movement and encourage them to learn them through making the movements themselves. In this way, a child comes to feel and understand what it means to walk or run or tiptoe and will not forget or mix up the words.

From walking age, children can begin to learn a selection of movements by making them along with adults or older children. You could say, 'Let's all walk together', and play a piece of appropriate music, taking children by the hand and walking jauntily around the room. Then repeat the exercise with other movements.

Walking quickly and slowly and beginning to stamp may be enough for very young toddlers. Two-year-olds will enjoy walking, running, jumping, stamping and dancing. Three- and four-year-olds will be willing to try a whole range of movements. Although many will not actually be able to hop or skip correctly before the age of 5, they should know what it means to hop or skip, be able to recognise when others are hopping or skipping and be able to make a good attempt at the correct movement when asked to hop or skip or when they wish to practise the skill for themselves in their play.

LEARNING THROUGH OPPOSITES AND CONTRASTS

Children love opposites and extremes. They like to imagine huge giants and tiny mice, running foxes and creeping snails, tall mountains and short grass, hard rocks and soft teddies, floating feathers and heavy bricks, balancing a sheet of paper on one hand or pushing a heavy wheelbarrow, digging a big hole and dropping in a tiny seed, splashing through a deep river or balancing across on stepping stones. Encourage this interest and use its learning potential by setting up situations where they can explore similarities and differences and act out contrasting movements and body shapes. Work on a different set of opposites in each session or each week of sessions, returning to each pair in a regular or random order. Opposites that you could offer might be:

> fast/slow; loud/quiet; big/small; tall/short; hard/soft; heavy/light; climbing up/slipping down; falling asleep/waking up.

Find two pieces of contrasting music which suggest to you the opposites, or use two percussion instruments on which you can play contrasting sounds.

Explain to the children that when they hear the first sound they should make the first type of movement and when they hear the second sound they should change their movement to fit. When first introducing this activity, demonstrate for them, join in with them and let them practise until you are sure that they all understand. Then allow them plenty of space and let them work alone, while you play the music or make the sounds

Emphasise that there is no one right movement for 'fast' or 'slow' – any type of movement that is fast or slow with any part or parts of the body is correct and the movements could be different each time the sound changes, or could stay the same. Some children may choose to copy others while their confidence is still gradually developing, and some small groups of children may choose to make the same movements as their friends, but independence and individual creativity should be encouraged and praised whenever seen.

Towards the end of the foundation stage, children may be able to demonstrate their movements for the class to watch and try to copy. This is a good way of rewarding a child who has worked very hard and would love to show his or her work to others, but avoid embarrassing a child who does not like to be the centre of attention or he/she may deliberately not try so hard next time! Ensure that all children are praised and that each child has a chance to show work to the class at some time over a term or similar period of sessions. Less confident children or those who prefer not to be in the limelight may be happy to show their work as a part of a small group rather than individually. Children who are working at an advanced level in movement skills may be ready to try working co-operatively with one or more friends to create a movement as a small group.

LISTENING SKILLS

Working with opposites and contrasts requires children to listen and react to what they hear. Listening skills are a vitally important area of learning for young children to develop. If they can listen carefully, take in and process information and then act on it, they will be able to move forward in all other areas of development. Just as a child who has difficulties with hearing must receive help to avoid missing out on development, so too must a child who has difficulties with listening and understanding, since hearing words is not enough if you do not know what they mean or how they affect you.

In dance and drama, listening skills can be easily practised in enjoyable ways. Games such as Musical Bumps and Musical Statues can be adapted to fit any theme in a session. Younger children love to dance to music and sit down when it stops. Slightly older ones love to freeze like statues. The game can become as complicated as you wish – try:

> dance to the music and, when it stops, sit down, put your seat belt on and drive your car; *or* dance to the music and, when it stops, stand very

Figure 14 Listening skills can be developed through games involving music, movement and dance.

still on one leg with one finger on your nose and the other hand on your head; *or* dance to the music and, when it stops, quack like a duck!

These games can be used to allow children to make a noise and use lots of space again after a quiet activity, or to allow them to move more gently after a boisterous action song. They require less concentration than learning a new skill or remembering the words of a song or rhyme, so are ideal to bring some light-hearted smiles and giggles back into the session. somewhere around the middle point.

Young children are wonderful when they dance freely to popular music – the spontaneous movements they make with their bodies complement the mixture of concentration, expectation and glee on their faces – and few parents and practitioners can resist joining in with them!

DANCE

Formal dance training is available to children, if their parents and carers want it, in a variety of different dance schools and groups and in some primary and nursery schools. Most dance teachers will accept children from the age of 3, or just before, and run special 'playdance' classes to introduce them to dance classes. As they grow older, the opportunities are endless; ballet, tap, jazz dance, disco, modern, gym dance, street, line dance, hip hop, etc.!

The benefits of sharing an interest in dance with others in a class, learning correct techniques, taking exams, performing onstage and loyally pursuing an activity with other teachers and classmates, away from the weekly routine of school or nursery, can be tremendous. All children, both boys and girls equally, can benefit from this excellent source of exercise, discipline and friendship.

But not all children will be able to dance in their leisure time and not all will want to. Many will have other, different hobbies and many families do not have the time or the resources to make such a commitment for their children. All children should have the opportunity to explore dance as a part of their daily lives as they are growing up, along with sport, artistic and academic activities.

This is why we must provide them with the opportunities for dance, as well as drama, speechwork, mime and movement, in their schools, pre-schools, nurseries and local groups and classes. Any rhythmic movement, inspired by music or a beat, made by a child can be called dance.

Chapter 7

Speech and language

We live in a world that relies totally on communication. Children need to be able to communicate with others without frustration, to enjoy creating and following through their own ideas and to be able to understand and participate within any project as a member of a group. Clear speech and good language skills are an asset and acquiring, developing and practising them can be fun.

ENUNCIATING IN UNISON

Enunciation is the art of speaking clearly and precisely and something that all actors and singers work on. There are many sounds, chants and exercises used by adults to facilitate and maintain good enunciation, but young children can learn and practise their speech skills enjoyably, through the saying of sentences, rhymes and songs together.

Gather the children around you in a circle or a group and tell them that you are going to do some 'special talking' together. Then, tell them that special talking is called 'enunciation'. Ask them to repeat the word with you and after you, as a group. It is a word that young children love to say and chant and they find it no more difficult or unusual than a word such as 'ballet' or 'trampolining'. At each subsequent session, announce that it is time for 'special talking' and ask the children what it should be called. Within a few sessions, even the 2- and 3-year-olds will be calling out the answer.

Either at the same time, or a few weeks later, tell the children that when we all speak together and at the same time it is called speaking 'in unison'. They usually find this even easier to remember and happily begin to tell the adults at home that they have been 'enunciating in unison' again today. This never fails to impress parents and other family members, but is, in fact, what young children naturally spend a lot of their time doing anyway, by choice when they are playing and with encouragement to help them to learn facts, safety rules and new ideas.

Choose a selection of well-known nursery rhymes and work on a different one at each session. First, ask the children whether they have heard of the rhyme. At least some will always say that they have. Ask them to listen to it carefully first, then either say it clearly yourself or play a good example of it from a children's tape or CD. You may have to insist that they do listen quietly, as some of the more confident and enthusiastic children may want to join in immediately. Explain to them that it is important that everybody in the class listens and thinks quietly first, as some may be hearing it for the first time and some rhymes are said differently in some verses by different people. After listening, agree on a version that everybody will use today.

Children enjoy 'warming their mouths up', by opening and shutting them and rubbing them with their fingers. When they have done this, ask the whole group to say the rhyme along with you. Maintain leadership of this, speaking slowly, clearly and loudly enough to encourage everybody to stay with you. It is a good idea to repeat the exercise at least once, speaking a little more quickly as the group's confidence grows.

RECOGNISING AND PREDICTING SPEECH

A group containing enough older children (of 3½ to 4 years upwards) will always enjoy filling in the words the leader 'forgets' and correcting the 'mistakes' he or she makes. This game requires good listening skills and builds on earlier activities involving contrasting sounds and reacting to silences.

First, introduce a well-known rhyme and allow the whole group to listen to it. Then let them practise enunciating it in unison. Once they are all confident of the rhyme and its words and rhythm, you can play slightly more advanced games.

Tell the children that you would like to be able to say the rhyme again on your own, but that you are a bit forgetful and you might need them to help you if you get stuck. Ask them whether they will help and most will agree enthusiastically. Begin to say the rhyme again, but stop and look puzzled just before certain key words. For example:

Baa baa black –
Have you any –
Yes sir, yes –
Three bags –

Encourage children to fill in the missing words, praising and thanking them all, and particularly the ones who come in first or remember a word that most of the others could not get.

You are likely to hear some very amusing words at times with this game, as some children may have misheard certain words in favourite nursery rhymes during their earlier years. It is fine to laugh with the children, so long as you never laugh at them or make them feel that what they said was wrong or silly, and the adults will enjoy remembering the jokes when they are away from the children.

When the group is proficient at filling in missing words, the game can be taken further. Instead of leaving puzzled gaps, speak the rhyme carefully but deliberately, say quite the wrong word at key moments and then pause when the children call out to you that you are wrong. For example:

Humpty Dumpty sat on a chair
Humpty Dumpty had a great jump
All the king's monkeys
And all the king's babies
Couldn't put Humpty to bed!

Young children love this game and, through playing it, they are learning to listen critically, to distinguish right from wrong or likely from unlikely and to react quickly and confidently without knowing that that is what they are doing. It also makes them laugh and that pulls everybody in the room together to work as a team and enjoy the session.

TAKING CUES

When they fill in missing words or replace incorrect words, the children are taking cues. Whenever you feel that they are ready to absorb more new vocabulary, tell them that that is what they are doing. Ask them if they would please listen for the 'cue', which is what another person says or does just before they should speak, and then 'take their cue' and speak the correct word or line at the correct time.

Once they understand this and have practised it with the previous games, children aged 4 and 5 should be able to play at 'passing the rhyme around'. Ask them to sit in a circle with you, so that they can easily see when it will be their turn. Start the game by saying one line of a rhyme. Ask the child seated beside you to say the next line and the child seated beside him or her to continue. If the rhyme is short and ends before each player has taken their turn, it should be said again from the beginning, the first line following on immediately after the last line. Try this with various rhymes of different lengths, passing around the circle in both directions and with children seated in different places at each session.

When each child has spoken and the rhyme reaches its starting point again, either say the last line(s) yourself or suggest that everybody says them together. Then praise the children for taking their cues so well and enunciating so clearly. You can now explain that this was, of course, not enunciating in unison, it was enunciating individually.

If any child is unable or unwilling to speak up when it is their turn, it does not help to put pressure on the child to do so. Allow enough seconds for natural hesitation, thinking or the summoning of courage, then ask the child by name whether they know the next line. If they don't know it, but would like to speak, gently remind them of the words and then allow them their turn and praise them for achieving the enunciation. If they do know the line, but are not prepared to speak out, ask whether they would like to speak with you or with the child next to them. If not, say the line yourself and pass on to the next child without any further comment. Give these children the same chance to participate at each session and they will suddenly do so one day when they feel ready and confident enough.

ACTING OUT

Once you have explored a rhyme and all its words and meanings in order to use it as an enunciation exercise, children will welcome the opportunity to act it out, especially if it is usually sung and you have a good version of it available on tape or CD to act and sing along to. Discuss together how to create the various characters and portray what they do and how they feel, then fit actions and mimes along to the song, singing as much as possible.

Nursery rhymes are usually sung quite quickly, so be prepared to act out a whole sequence in a few seconds and stress that this is part of the

Figure 15 Children enjoy creating characters and actions to fit favourite songs and rhymes.

fun of this particular activity. It is a good idea to find or record the song sung at least two or three times, not just once, as your rapid actions may otherwise pass in a blur and the children may not feel satisfied that they really did act out the rhyme.

PROJECTION OF THE VOICE

If you have a stage that the children can stand on, or a designated area that you use for performing as though to an audience, obviously you will have discussed with the children that this is a good place to use their enunciation skills. They will also be able to practise their cue taking if they stand onstage in a line or a group and take turns to speak out.

Explain to them that enunciation makes up half of the important way we speak onstage. The other half comes from being able to project your voice to an audience, so that they can hear you clearly even if they are some distance away. Older children may be able to grasp the idea of sound waves coming out of their mouths, hitting the wall at the back of the hall or room and falling down over the audience. Teach children to take a breath and push their voices out, speaking slightly more slowly and slightly more loudly than usual, but not shouting, and remembering to enunciate.

If they are speaking in unison, encourage them to maintain a sensible speed and not to slow down and wait for each other until the speech becomes a mournful chant! If they are speaking individually, encourage them each to find their own comfortable speed and style of speaking and to take cues confidently.

It is possible for children to learn to do this and to enjoy the experience of performing to an invited audience of their own families and friends from the age of 3 years, provided that they have an adequate level of support and encouragement from practitioners throughout the experience and that the whole event is carefully planned and monitored to run smoothly but flexibly, putting the needs of the children first.

In regular classes and group sessions, allow time for conversations and discussions, as this enriches language development. Young children's vocabularies increase at an astonishing rate and their pronunciation and understanding of words can only improve through practice. Model correct speech yourself at all times, taking care to enunciate clearly and to project your own voice to lead activities, rather than shouting. When children become noisy and excited, and it is time to change to a quieter activity, one loudly projected request to stop and gather around, followed by soft speech or whispers to those who come to join in is very effective in calming and refocusing the group.

Naturally demonstrate, through your own example, different forms of correct speech for different situations. Enunciation during rhymes, projection onstage and conversational language used when chatting within a group require subtle differences in approach that children can only learn and absorb through planned and shared experiences with caring and interested adults. Be careful to listen properly to children's spontaneous speech and to make appropriate comments and replies, proving your interest and demonstrating the correct 'give and take' nature of conversations. This is an important life skill that children can learn most easily through imitation.

SPECIAL NEEDS

A child who has a hearing and/or a speech impairment may have difficulty with some speech and language activities, but you should always aim to make them accessible to everybody. One-to-one support may be needed in some cases and this could be provided by an adult or, sometimes, by a caring and sensible child.

Chanting and singing will aid the development of enunciation and encourage a child to form words more quickly to maintain a rhythm. They can also help a child who often feels isolated to feel accepted and welcomed within a group, as singing is an excellent social experience that encourages people to come together, regardless of their similarities or differences.

All attempts to communicate with you or with others in the group should be praised and encouraged. Even a child with little coherent speech should feel able and eager to join in when the group speaks, through sounds or a sign language or a combination of the two.

Wherever possible, early years practitioners, teachers and support staff should familiarise themselves with basic signs (both British Sign Language and Makaton, as well as any particular signs that a specific child in their care uses), but also accept a parent, carer, keyworker or learning support Assistant as a translator when this will help a child to communicate more effectively. Signing can include a rich use of language and vocabulary and allow a child a chance to speak to others, displaying intelligence and imagination, despite their disability.

Children who do not have English as their first language can benefit from all drama and language activities in the same way as their peers, but will particularly increase their understanding and use of the language through listening to stories, chanting rhymes, singing songs and matching mimes and actions to words. They may also participate in sessions with an adult or another child to assist in translation as necessary. Or, in private classes, a child may even attend with a parent or relative who has little experience of English and become the translator in their turn.

Chapter 8

Rhythm and singing

From birth, babies enjoy being sung to by adults and older children, and listening to live or recorded music and singing. As they grow up, children enjoy singing along to favourite tunes and joining in with familiar songs and rhymes with families and friends, teachers and carers and groups of other children. While children must have quiet times for rest and concentration and should not be distracted by the constant background noise of a television or radio which nobody is watching or listening to, a tape or CD playing children's songs or music that is easy to listen to can often provide a calmer and happier atmosphere for free play than complete silence. Children may then choose to sing or dance along at times, or just listen as they build, create and interact with each other.

Although many parents will share songs with their children at home, they will also expect them to learn others and experience singing and rhythm activities within their peer group in a nursery or school setting, or take them to private groups and classes especially for this experience.

START WITH FAMILIAR SONGS

By the time they enter the foundation stage, most children will have experienced some songs with their families or regular carers. Try to find out which songs are already particular favourites and begin your singing sessions with those.

If they are not able to remember any songs by name, guess at some and begin to sing or play them. It will be obvious which children are familiar with them, as they will smile in recognition and begin to join in with the singing or bounce along to the rhythm.

Nursery rhymes are introduced to children because they are fun to learn and sing together and easy to remember, although some of the words are old-fashioned and some of the rhymes unusual. Sometimes, they can demand quite a wide voice range to sing well, but young children will not worry about getting the tune perfectly correct and will happily join in with their own approximations. They are also an important part of our heritage and our history and a part of childhood that has been shared by many generations. Other nursery songs have also become popular over the years, many with repetitive actions and choruses, that relate to children's everyday experiences.

If you are a confident singer you may prefer to sing unaccompanied, or you may enjoy singing along with tapes or CDs, especially if the songs you choose include interesting backing music, tune variations or harmonies. If you do not sing confidently, you may feel happier with the support of a simple recorded version of a song, or you may find it easier to start a song and encourage the children to take over with their voices, just maintaining the timing and rhythm with them, to keep them singing together. Remember that young children are not judgemental, and, although they may come to realise that they really enjoy listening to a particular adult sing or feel especially inspired by them, they will appreciate everybody's efforts and never decide that somebody 'can't sing'. It is important that all adults involved with the children understand this and ensure that no child ever feels or says 'I can't sing' because somebody has said such a thing to them or within their hearing. You don't have to have a voice of a standard to perform a solo in a concert to enjoy singing as a group activity!

Using familiar songs and rhymes ensures that the adults in the group, whether childcare practitioners, teachers, carers or parents, will all know them and feel confident enough to join in and lead and encourage the children to do so. It is extremely useful for any group or class leader or practitioner or teacher in a setting to have a repertoire of familiar songs and rhymes that the children enjoy singing and chanting together. They can be used to open or close a session, bring a group back together if they seem to be drifting apart or warn children that it is about to be time for the next part of a setting's routine, such as a mealtime or time to go outside.

TEACHING NEW SONGS

If you have chosen a new song that you would like to introduce to the children, tell them about it with enthusiasm and introduce it at a time when they are receptive to learning something new – not when they are tired or hungry, or have just spent an extended period concentrating on other new or demanding activities or have been sitting still for too long. Explain a little about the song first, but avoid complicated background information, which would be inappropriate for this age group. The children might be interested to know if a particular character or animal or type of person usually sings the song, or if it tells a story or describes a feeling or reminds us of some simple rules. Always tell them that you like the song and that you would like to share it with them and hope that they will like it too.

Either play a recorded version of the song to the children or sing it to them, unaccompanied or with an instrument if you play one. The ability to play a piano or a guitar can enhance a singing experience for the group, as it allows the teacher to sing along.

Instruments that must be blown can be used to help to teach a tune in the early stages of learning a song. But young children are unable to sing along to them, as their ability to maintain rhythm and timing varies too much without a strong leading voice. It is best to sit close to the children and maintain eye contact with them while singing and playing. Percussion instruments, such as tambourines, small drums, bells or maracas can be very helpful in establishing a strong rhythm, but be aware that, if you play one, the children will all want to play one too, so be prepared to arrange a music session for them now or later, or to pass the instrument around and let them all take a turn.

Unless the song is very short, teach a part of it at a time, starting with the simplest part or the chorus that repeats, if there is one. When the children have listened to the song once or twice, sing a line at a time for them and ask them to sing it back to you or sing it again with you. Repeat any line that is hard to learn until the majority of the singers can manage it. When they have mastered four lines or one simple verse or chorus, put it all together and sing it as a group. After working on each new part, return to the chorus or the part that you all know well, to ensure that the children's self confidence remains high. Give lots of praise for the effort and progress they are making and the good sounds that are being achieved. Very young children enjoy giving themselves a clap or three cheers when they have done well and are thrilled when their special adults do this for or with them.

Introduce a new song over more than one session and allow children to 'warm up' and 'cool down' with more well-known ones, working on the new one in the middle of a singing session. It will gradually become so familiar that the children will no longer see it as a new song. Once they all know it well, it is fun to remind them of how short a time ago they did not know it at all. It is then time to introduce another new song and ask the children to remember how easily they learned the previous one.

This means that each new song is likely to be approached with a greater and greater confidence, as they begin to realise the potential learning ability at their command. If children firmly believe that they can do something, they usually can!

FAVOURITES

Note which songs are particular favourites with the children and return to them just often enough to make sure that they remain favourites – not the songs we have all become bored with! Older nursery and reception class aged children will enjoy taking turns to choose a song, and may even like to sing a part of their favourite song to the rest of the group before everybody sings it together. If you are going to encourage this, do make sure that turns are taken fairly and that each child is offered the opportunity to choose or perform within a suitable time period. It is better to look at your group and ask one or more children by name to select a song than to ask 'Who would like to choose a song for us?' Open ended questions and offers like that, with this age group, result in the loudest, boldest and most confident children taking a turn almost every time, whilst quieter or less confident children, or those who take a little longer to think about the question, may always be overlooked and never develop the desire to lead or even participate fully.

IN A NURSERY OR SCHOOL SETTING

You will usually be able to keep all your resources and materials in an appropriate room or area and use them as you wish. Although you will have planned your sessions and may be bringing in resources of your own from time to time, favourite songs should be available to you whenever you need them and whenever you can be flexible within your timetable.

If you are working on a theme, but you suddenly remember a song which will fit with a particular child's present interest or enthusiasm, you should aim to introduce it quickly, to respond to the interest and allow it to develop further before it wanes. Any interest that a young child has will probably be shared with at least a few others in his or her peer group and can become the beginning of a stimulating topic for the group to explore.

If you, the leader of the activity, are a confident and accomplished singer, do share your love of singing with all the children and the other staff. Don't be afraid to add harmonies and variations to simple tunes and to explore a wide variety of songs. Children and adults enjoy listening to somebody sing for pleasure and a live performance, either unaccompanied or with a 'backing track', is a treat. You can be sure that at least some of the children, and maybe other staff too, will be inspired and go on to sing for pleasure themselves, always remembering with fondness who first introduced them to singing.

IN PRIVATE CLASSES

Each session will be carefully planned in advance and only the appropriate resources will be available at each one, but it should still be possible to be a little flexible. If a child or parent requests a particular song that has become a favourite, perhaps from a previous term, you will probably have to say that you don't have it with you or can't fit it in today but that you will try to include it next week or within the next two or three weeks. There should always be room for flexibility within your planned themes and activities to respond to a child's area of specific interest or enjoyment as soon as possible, either by adding an extra item or swapping it for one which can as easily be used at another point in the future. Anything that makes a child or family feel special and valued by the class leader is important.

If you have chosen to run musical drama classes for children privately, it is quite likely that you will be somebody who loves to sing. Make the most of this and share your enjoyment with the children, parents and carers in your classes. Choose songs that fit the range of your singing voice and that you particularly like to sing, and perform each number confidently to your audience. There can be no greater encouragement to join in than a good singer happily and confidently leading and sharing a good song.

You will often find that some of the adults who have chosen to attend these classes with their children are doing so because they enjoy singing themselves. They may also have good voices and be thrilled at the opportunity to use them to sing along with you each week. Consider which new songs you could introduce that would be interesting and challenging to them as well as to the children.

When parents, grandparents, nannies and childminders spontaneously tell you how much fun they are having, and ask where they can get copies of some of the songs you are using to listen to at home, you know that you are getting it right. There is absolutely no need for young children's activities to be boring for the adults involved. Since it is the adults who must make the commitment to attending regularly and paying for the classes, it is sensible to ensure that they will be glad to do so. Special times that allow adults and their children to share and develop their skills together are valuable for their relationships, as well as for the learning that takes place.

BUSY TIMES AND QUIET TIMES

Alternate busy action songs and boisterous dance numbers or ring games with quieter songs and the chanting of rhythmic rhymes. Children need to understand that there are many different ways of singing and that some people may find one type easier or more enjoyable than another. There should be plenty of opportunities for them to find and explore their voices.

It can be fun to include work on opposites and contrasts within singing activities. Ask the children to sing:

- as loudly as they can and then as softly as they can;
- in a jerky voice and then in a smooth voice;
- in a voice that gets gradually louder or gradually softer;
- in a cross voice or a pleased voice;
- in a character's voice – e.g. a baby, an old person, an angry troll, a lion, a snake, etc.

If you think that the children are ready to learn more describing words, then offer them *piano* and *forte*, *staccato* and *legatto*, *crescendo* and *diminuendo* as you work on them.

Some songs specifically teach children about 'loud and soft' or 'happy and cross'. Many others can be adapted by an experienced practitioner to do so.

SONGS TO TEACH IMPORTANT LESSONS

Because singing is an enjoyable and teambuilding activity, it is the ideal medium for teaching other lessons that children may be learning.

Singing along is one of the easiest ways to plant words, numbers, phrases and ideas in the memory. Music, singing and rhythmic chanting have been used extensively in the teaching of modern languages, historical facts and times-tables and other mathematical rules to older children.

Young children can enjoy and learn from singing songs in other languages, especially if they are languages spoken by families attending the setting. They may also enjoy helping to adapt their own class or group rules to fit a well-known tune, or basic sums, spellings or movement words. Acting out the words as they are sung further reinforces messages.

There are many tapes and CDs available containing songs that cover every aspect of care and learning for a young child. If you would like to remind them of anything from 'feeling special' to 'saying please and thank you' or 'being a good friend', you should know of or be able to find a song to suit the situation.

RHYTHM

The art of hearing, understanding and responding to rhythm involves other activities as well as singing. Even people who are determined that they cannot or will not sing can tap out a rhythm, or play instruments very successfully, or dance beautifully or move in a rhythmic way. Children need opportunities to explore rhythm separately from speech and singing and should be encouraged to develop skills and confidence in this area.

Moving to a beat played on a percussion instrument or to music allows children to hear and feel a rhythm and respond to it in a natural way. By the age of 3 or 4, most children should be able to listen to a rhythm and recognise when a walking movement would fit better than running, or marching would be more appropriate than tiptoeing, or how fast or slow a jumping or hopping movement should be. Dancing freely to music of many different types will allow children to try out new ways of expressing themselves and develop the ability to fit their own movements to the rhythm they hear.

Playing along to songs with a variety of percussion instruments also develops abilities in rhythm, provided that the children are encouraged to listen and think about what they are hearing and singing. Songs involving clapping or hammering, stamping or marching tend to have very strong rhythms that can be easily recognised and copied, as do nursery rhymes. Demonstrate for children how to say or clap a rhythm and then repeat it with the instrument. Play and sing along with them, leading strongly with both your instrument and your voice. Allow them to practise as many times as they like. Return to familiar songs frequently and praise children who make efforts to emulate what they hear with a variety of instruments at each session. This activity must be led firmly and confidently by the adult, to keep children on task and ensure that some learning can take place. Free play with instruments may be offered as a separate activity at another time.

Children nearing the end of the foundation stage may be able to extend their work on rhythm to creating whole songs or tunes as a group. They could sit in a circle or a line and take turns to clap or play a small part of the song each, taking their cues and moving on from each other as they might have learned in speech and language activities.

Or they might create a short performance of a well known or made up rhythm, working co-operatively within a very small group, and show it to their classmates. Children who are working at an advanced level may like

Figure 16 Older children can practice rhythm by clapping and stamping the beat of a song, for others to copy or guess.

to copy a rhythm that you play or clap and stamp for them, or play or clap and stamp the rhythm of a song for you and the rest of the group to identify. They may even move on to copying and guessing rhythms within pairs or small groups independently, without your direct supervision or leadership, or choose to bring this into their own play at other times.

AN EXTENSIVE REPERTOIRE

A crucial resource for any practitioner working in drama or music with young children is the knowledge of and the ability to remember, find and use a vast number of varied musical numbers. Sometimes you will plan what to use over an extended period (long-term planning), and sometimes you will develop ideas as you work on topics and see which areas are of most interest and stimulation to the children (medium-term planning). But there will also be times when you see that you can suddenly enhance your provision with an appropriate song, or you need to fill an unexpected five-minute 'gap' with a constructive and enjoyable activity for the whole group, or you need to bring your group together to re-focus but they are too wriggly for a quiet story (short-term planning).

Collect songs from everywhere, all the time. If you hear a song playing that immediately suggests a use to you, or that you just think you might like to use in the future, always find out what it is and arrange to buy or borrow a copy of it.

If themes, ideas or songs come into your head at an unusual moment, write them down as soon as you possibly can and look carefully at your notes later. This may mean that your planning is suddenly almost completed for a future term.

It is possible to find songs to fit a theme or to find a theme to fit songs. Never discard any song that you have used already or that you think you might not use after all. They take up almost no space – keep them all in case. You might suddenly find the perfect use for a song years after you collected it, or be able to exchange one with another practitioner who has different ideas or is working with a different age group.

If you have literally thousands of songs at your fingertips – in a neat array of clearly labelled tapes or CDs, in your head and on the tip of your tongue – you can be confident that you will always be able to plan well-structured musical, rhythmic and dramatic learning, or provide some constructive fun with no notice at all.

Chapter 9

Taking turns

All children need to learn how and when to take turns with others. Throughout our lives, we continue to need this ability. Adults of all ages know how to take turns to speak in conversations, to form queues in shops and to wait for buses, to sit in waiting rooms until they are called for appointments and to find appropriate ways and times to achieve their desires without upsetting other people. There are few things more irritating to most of us than the person who 'jumps a queue' or continuously interrupts with his or her own views and never listens properly to anybody else. These people will find themselves without the friends and career and life possibilities that they could have had if they were more able to make themselves acceptable to the majority. So it is important to give our children the necessary skills and not deny them the chance to learn them.

Very young children see themselves as the centre of the world and have no concept of others having equal rights or of the need to learn to share and take turns with them. But they are capable of learning very gradually from a young age, provided they have lots of opportunities to practise the required skills and lots of positive encouragement, reminders and reinforcements from the adults and older children that they associate with. Drama provides many varied opportunities for taking turns and a good practitioner will make the most of all of them as they arise.

TAKING CUES

When standing onstage or sitting or standing in a line or a circle on the floor, children can see clearly how to take their turn after the person to one side of them and before the person to the other side. This is the simplest way of learning to take cues. Older children will be able to move on to taking cues and speaking in turn from a script, provided they have practised turn taking as a younger child.

Ask children to choose where to sit or stand and then ask them to look carefully at the people who are next to them. Make sure they understand which direction the cue will be taken from – who speaks before whom and after whom – and let them practise speaking in turn. You may need to prompt most of the children by name the first time, gradually moving on to pointing or nodding at the ones who don't come in, until the whole group can manage to concentrate and participate in the activity without direct help. In this way, children can feel and understand with their bodies and their voices how to wait for their turn to come and then confidently take the turn at the right moment, knowing that others will listen to them as they have listened. Explain to them that this is called 'waiting for your cue' and 'taking your cue' – more 'stage talk' that they will love.

When children are seated in a circle or a group for a drama activity, they can be encouraged to share and discuss ideas with you and each other. Try some simple themes at first and increase the complexity as your group become more experienced and confident speakers. Make it clear to them that their ideas are interesting and important to you and to the others in the group and that they may choose to say anything that they think is relevant.

Mime opening an exciting birthday present in a big box and ask children in turn to tell you what is inside. Some will choose toys or sweets, while those who have developed greater skills in imagination might think up something unusual, such as 'a baby tiger' or 'a pink monkey', or something that wouldn't really fit into a box, such as 'a blue whale' or 'a combine harvester', and enjoy making you and the other children laugh or be surprised.

Mime walking through a jungle or forest and pretend to see a scary creature, then ask children in turn which creature they saw. Some will think logically about the dramatic setting and say an animal that might be found in a jungle, such as a lion or a snake, or in a forest, such as a bear or a wolf, while some will think more dramatically and choose a fantasy creature, such as a dragon or a giant. Some will just focus on what might scare them and believe that it would be possible to find a crocodile in a forest or a goose in a jungle.

There are no wrong answers! Remember that the purpose of this activity is actually to teach children to wait for their turn, listen to others and then speak out confidently to the group. Work on a mime or action song activity involving building a tower or a wall, then ask children in turn:

How high was your tower, Amelia?
or What did you use to build your tower, Chelsea?
or What did you use to stick the bricks together for your wall, Anjali?

While a few children nearing the end of the foundation stage might try to describe the height of a tower in standard or non-standard units, such as centimetres or handspans, younger ones will say that their tower was 'as high as the sky', or 'up to the clouds', or 'as big as an elephant', or 'as tall as Daddy'. This is a correct response and dramatic and expressive similies should be very much encouraged.

It is very interesting to note which children always choose sensible, logical answers, such as bricks or boxes to build a tower or a wall and cement or glue to stick them together, and which children always choose something imaginative, such as 'bouncy cushions' or 'spiky hedgehogs' stuck together with honey or golden syrup. Some will vary from day to

Figure 17 Children love to show the group the tower they have built, or describe the roof they have made.

day, depending on their mood. This can offer you an insight into the type of personality a child has and can be particularly helpful in speeding up the making of relationships with new children and the meeting of their individual needs when you only see them for an hour or two once a week.

As children grow older and more experienced, try asking them to imagine and discuss their ideas before acting them out, rather than afterwards. This requires more advanced thinking skills. Again, the focus of the activity is on waiting, listening and taking a turn appropriately, but the range of ideas can be celebrated too.

Ask each child in turn to tell everybody which jungle animal they will be. Then let them all act out the animals together at the same time. Or ask each child in turn to describe their favourite piece of play equipment in the park and then let them all act out the movements that they would use to play on the equipment.

The oldest children and those working at an advanced level in turn-taking and mime skills may be able to take turns to make a suggested or chosen expression to the child next to them or to mime or act out an animal or an action in turn for the rest of the group to guess or copy.

LISTENING TO EACH OTHER

There are few more appreciated skills in the world than that of being a good listener. People who can be relied upon to really listen and take in what others are saying, offering real support and only appropriate help in difficult or confusing situations, are much sought after as counsellors and the type of strong friends that everybody wants to have.

Listening to others is also an important part of good manners and shows courtesy for the rights and feelings of those around you. Shouting out answers instead of putting up a hand or waiting to be asked, or offering an opinion without waiting for the speaker to finish or indicating your wish to comment, is behaviour that is frowned upon and not expected in normal circumstances. But the appropriate behaviour skills and the need for them must be learned in early childhood and practised until they may be used confidently in any situation.

Begin by teaching the children to listen to you. In most situations, there needs to be a leader who explains to everybody else what is going to happen or what is required of them and asks then whether they understand, whether they agree or whether they have any problems. Other adults must stop talking or fidgeting and listen to what the leader says once the session begins, to set the right example for the children, and they should also help and encourage all the children to pay attention and stop distracting others.

Young children may not yet know that listening to somebody when they have something important to say or when they have been placed in authority is the correct thing to do, but they can learn it very easily, if they experience a consistent environment where adults and children respect each other.

When you ask a child a question, use the child's name and indicate by the tone of voice you use that this child has been chosen to speak and everybody should listen to him or her for the next few moments. Promote good listening skills by ensuring that each child has a turn to speak and is not hurried or corrected. If a child is not yet ready to speak alone, they may choose to take their turn by whispering to you or to another adult or child or simply indicating that they do not wish to speak today. This child should never be forced to say something or made to feel inadequate because of their decision, but offered the same chance again, without fuss, at each session until he or she chooses to participate. And, when the great day comes, praise the child for the contribution but don't go 'over the top' or you may undo the confidence that has been so newly gained.

Maintain eye contact with the speaking child throughout each turn, proving that you are listening and taking a real interest in what is being said. Encourage the other children to look towards the speaker too (without staring too much) and to sit or stand still and quietly to avoid distracting others and missing vital words. Some children will look at the floor or their hands while they speak until their confidence increases, but work towards them looking at the person they are speaking to and using body language to further facilitate communication. A child who shouts out or interrupts when another child is speaking should be gently reminded that 'We are all enjoying hearing what Jemimah has to say at the moment, so could you please listen too? Then we will all hear what you have to tell us when it's your turn in a minute.'

Children still in the early stages of the foundation curriculum will not yet be able to wait and listen quietly for their turn and should not be expected to do it until they are mature enough.

All children interrupt at times when they become excited by or absorbed in the topic being discussed, or cause a distraction because they lose concentration and become bored or confused, and an explanation may be all that is needed. If a child is gradually learning to control more impulsive speech or behaviour, reminders over a few sessions will often get the message across without any further problems. A child who has definite difficulties in listening to others and waiting quietly for a turn to speak, possibly due to a special need, may need the support of a one-to-one adult beside him or her during the appropriate parts of a drama session in order to achieve the objective and not disrupt the session for the other children.

If a child confidently takes their turn but their speech is unclear and you are unable to understand what they say, you may be able to sensitively ask a parent or carer or the child's keyworker or another staff member if they understood. They may be more aware of the way the child forms certain words or sounds and be able to 'translate' for you, so that you don't miss the good idea that the child offered. If nobody understood, you could ask the child to repeat their idea once and try again. If you are still unsure, it may be best to pretend that you did understand and praise the child's contribution as usual! You may suddenly work it out much later in the day and be well prepared for the next session.

DISCUSSION OF IDEAS

Accept and praise all ideas equally, even if a child is helped to think or speak by an adult, but take especial note of which children think up lots of new ideas and which ones tend to copy the child beside them, the most popular idea or their best friend. Find opportunities to offer extra praise and encouragement to these very imaginative children and hope that more and more of the group may gradually try to emulate them.

Children may gradually begin to understand more subtle differences in whether or not it is appropriate to speak out or interrupt occasionally and when a whole group discussion would be more valuable than everybody listening to one person at length. For example, if one child says that they have found a favourite toy in a present or had a popular food for dinner, it may be satisfying to that child to hear one or more of the group agreeing that 'That's my favourite too' or 'I like that for dinner as well' and it will not disrupt the turn taking within the circle or line. If a child says that they like something and another mutters that they don't like it, this is only a problem if they say it in an unpleasant way or try to imply that the first child is wrong to hold a different opinion. It is valuable for children to learn that it is constructive for different people to like different things and that discussing likes and dislikes is just interesting.

Be prepared to flexibly initiate whole group discussions, including shows of hands or votes on who likes one thing more than another, whenever you feel that this would be appropriate, but ensure that individuals still get their chance to speak alone afterwards if they have been waiting for their turn. Children will only agree to wait patiently if they are secure in the knowledge that turns will be taken fairly and overseen by an adult who doesn't forget whose turn it was or who had waited without interrupting or fidgeting.

As in all areas of learning, take notice of how much progress each individual child is making, rather than their overall ability level, and avoid comparing them with each other. Children enter the foundation stage with widely differing levels of ability. Our task is to ensure that each one has the opportunity to progress further before moving on to the next stage.

Chapter 10

Working together as a team

Drama is essentially a sociable activity. When people act, sing, dance or perform in any way, they seldom do so alone, but are usually members of a group or team who work together to create a whole experience. And, of course, all performers are supported by other groups of people, such as backstage crews, production teams or orchestras. However large or small a person's contribution and whether or not they are seen 'in the limelight', they must see their role as a crucial part of their team's work and strive always to be conscientious and reliable and to get on constructively with those around them.

This applies to people of all ages, and the earlier this attitude is learned and embedded within a child's conscience and understanding the more successful the child will have a chance of being in later life, in whichever career path they choose, and also in their hobbies and personal life.

IN PRIVATE CLASSES

When you begin and end sessions you will draw all the children together into a circle. At other times, you may ask them to sit or stand in a line for particular activities, or gather them into a group for a story or discussion time. Children who know each other well will usually choose to sit beside each other at these times, especially when they do not yet know the others at all. It is important to be aware of which children see each other outside classes and to allow them to be together when appropriate. This may give them the necessary confidence boost to enable them to achieve high levels of involvement and embrace new challenges. Many people prefer to take a friend along with them to a new activity throughout their lives!

However, you must also note carefully which children display improved confidence and behaviour control in the presence of their friends and which do not. Some children may not be helped by the close proximity of certain others, although they are delighted to be with them! Much depends on the personality and previous experiences of each child. Some people are naturally good for each other, while others may successfully maintain their relationship in only certain situations. A confident pair or group of children may make each other too excited to concentrate, or may struggle with feelings of competition or rivalry. A less confident pair or group may increase each other's nervousness or be unable to work individually, always hesitating to express themselves and copying each other.

If you feel that certain children would be better working away from each other, you could suggest that they sit at either side of you at first and encourage them to make relationships with the children on their other sides. Then select those that you think they could get on well with or be helped by and sensitively manoeuvre them into situations where they find themselves close to those children as though accidentally. Monitor the situation carefully and praise children both for working with new friends and for working more sensibly and constructively with 'old' friends if they subsequently achieve this when they encounter them again. You may need to explain your feelings and your objectives and enlist the help of other practitioners or parents or carers as appropriate if this approach is to have the maximum desired effect.

Encourage children to be sensitive to others but quietly confident about what they would like to happen. They should come to the circle or group and choose an appropriate place for themselves. If a child becomes upset because they wish to sit beside a friend and there is no space there, you could politely ask another child if they would mind swapping places or ask all the children to shuffle round a little to make the desired space appear.

Work towards the children becoming confident enough to ask this for themselves. Praise the child who says: 'Please could you move up a little bit, Tia, so that I can sit next to Thomas?' *or* 'Can I swap places with you, Ellie, so that I can be with Dylan and you can be with Abigail?'

Thank the child who agrees and moves when they are asked or lets a child squeeze in beside them. Especially thank and praise the child who moves around or shuffles closer to another to solve a potential problem or who welcomes another child into the circle or group and offers a place for them to sit, without being asked.

Ensure that you take less confident children or those needing extra support or attending without a parent or carer to sit beside you as much as necessary, but don't let any one child come to expect that they have a divine right to that coveted spot forever, or that they should continue to rely on that level of support as their confidence grows. A steady stream of younger and newer children joining a class usually ensures that the older, more experienced ones can feel important in gradually managing more and more 'on their own'.

Your ultimate aim is for every child in the class to be happy to sit or stand beside whoever they find themselves next to by chance, to hold hands with them as required and to exchange chatty remarks in a friendly manner as appropriate. This is a very tall order that will seldom be completely achieved with children so young, but it is good to keep the overall ideal goal in mind and feel rewarded each time a child progresses a little further towards it, however gradual the advances of the group as a whole. In this way, you continuously contribute towards building the children's confidence, social skills and self-esteem.

Parents and carers may have joined a class together with friends or come along to join others that they know who already attend. They see their drama as a social activity and, although they are keen for their children to learn new skills, they want them to enjoy themselves and spend time with their friends. Ensure that there are a few minutes free for chatting here and there, between activities, and accept that the adults will want to chat too. Praise adults and children for joining in enthusiastically together and encourage everybody to work together, with you, as a team. If learning objectives are achieved, that's marvellous. If everybody has a good time, has fun and laughs together, that's wonderful too!

IN A NURSERY OR SCHOOL SETTING

All of the above applies equally to children in a nursery, pre-school or reception group or class while they are still new to each other. But, if they attend the setting every day or several times a week, they will become familiar with each other much more quickly and begin to work together as a team more easily in all situations, because they become very used to doing so.

Children may make progress more quickly in some group activities in these settings, but this may be offset by them moving on after a shorter period of time, while others may attend a private class for two years or more.

Teachers, nursery nurses, room leaders and keyworkers will be able to offer valuable insights into which children work together well and which are better separated. This can be discussed at length if necessary, out of the children's hearing. With the extra professional support of other qualified staff working with you during drama sessions, you may be able to gradually encourage and develop the abilities of all children to work together, to allow successful new pairings and groupings to emerge who can learn to co-operate under supervision. All staff must be consistent in their approach to participation, courtesy and standards of behaviour, following your lead during sessions and discussing any issues that arise or differences in opinion later when the children are not present.

Remember to praise staff members too! They will enjoy being appreciated when they turn in enthusiastic and accomplished performances to encourage the children in their care. Not all early years practitioners will see drama activities as their favourite part of the job, but, with the right encouragement and example, everybody can enjoy working together.

ACTING OUT STORIES

The best teamwork can often be observed when children and their adult carers or teachers act out a story together. Tell a story as simply as possible, or lead and guide a discussion on the storyline of a very well-known tale.

Choose a tale or a character that many of the children have had previous experience of, using a book with lots of pictures, a comic, magazine or poster, or some toys, models or objects to illustrate the important characters and events in the story. Then suggest that everybody acts it out together.

If a child stands up or shuffles around because they cannot see the pictures or objects well during a story, reassure them that they will each see in turn, or suggest where they might move to at this point while you wait, but never allow it to happen without comment and without resolving the problem immediately. If one child begins to break up the group in this way, the others will then be unable to see or concentrate either and will copy him or her and, within two minutes, the team and the activity will have dissolved.

If you stand up and launch into the first happening in the story with enthusiasm, everybody should feel inspired to follow you! Narrate the storyline as appropriate as your actions and expressions unfold, encouraging everybody to copy what you are doing, but not necessarily to imitate you exactly.

Figure 18 Acting out a simple story together develops children's imaginative and teamworking skills.

Praise every attempt you see to describe the story through actions, expressions, words, sounds and mimes, and every sensible or interesting addition to the plot or characters offered by a child or adult.

SEQUENCES

Undertaken in mime or with the addition of speech or sounds, these are very short 'mini stories' that children act out, either all together or in small groups for others to watch. Encourage children to look carefully at each other's work and to offer praise spontaneously if they see something that they particularly like.

Supporting each other through performing together for others to watch, or through being an appreciative or constructively critical audience, leads to the true feeling of being a member of a team and proud to be so.

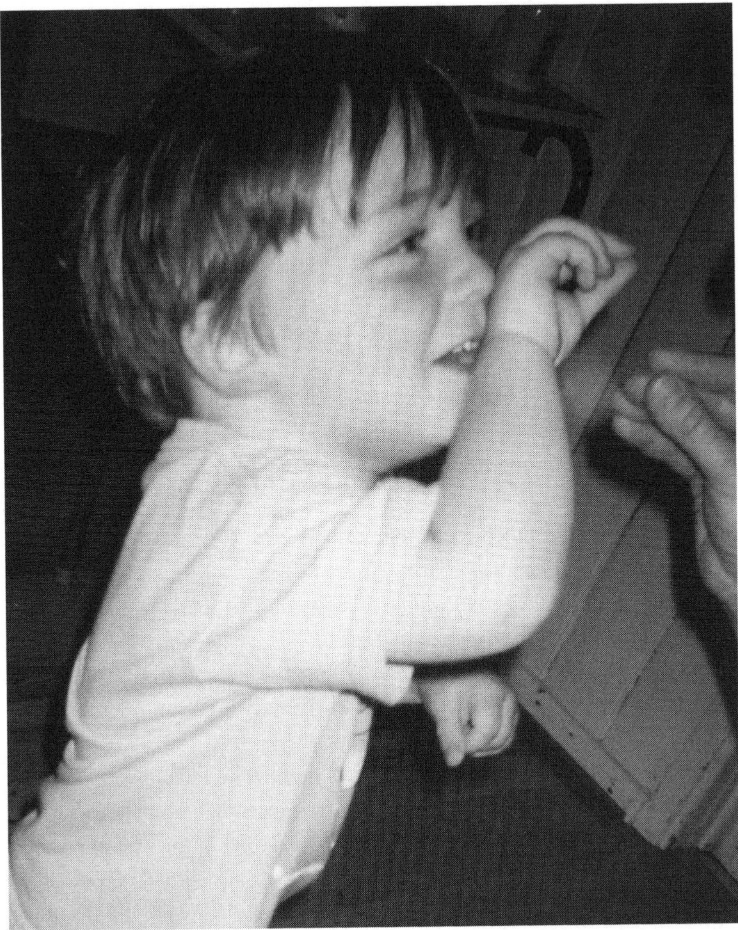

Figure 19 Encourage children to join in story-telling by copying your actions or by acting out elements of the story.

CELEBRATING DIFFERENCES

Although we do not want to encourage a culture of one child feeling that they are better than another, or one feeling inadequate because somebody else's performance is said to be more accomplished, a friendly atmosphere which includes some 'healthy competition' actually promotes better teamwork. If you ask 'Who can make the crossest face?' or 'Who can push the heaviest wheelbarrow?' everybody will put forth their best effort,

Figure 20 Children quickly understand how they can support each other through performing together.

giving you the opportunity to praise a few children (and adults) at a time. It is almost guaranteed that they will also become excited and laugh because they are now having fun.

Ensure that there are enough activities on offer to enable you to praise different people each time and that you have mentioned everybody's name at least once. Through a harmless feeling of 'I was one of the best at pushing a wheelbarrow, but my friend Isabella was better at making a cross face', or 'Rosie can jump higher, but Henry can hop for longer', children can come to understand and accept that we are all good at different things and that people like to be friends with us if we can express and celebrate our various achievements together.

As children grow older, life does become more competitive and this can be a good thing, if it is not taken too far. Competing with others can challenge us to make our very best efforts and give us the reward of feeling that we have done well.

Children need to learn how to win and how to lose, how to accept success or defeat gracefully, how to avoid feeling devastated when they don't come out on top, how to be pleased but modest when they do and how to join in with congratulating others on their successes. They need to know that team players should not gloat over others or feel angry with them and that the most important thing is to be a good sport who plays fairly. Confident people who take pride in their achievements but take care of other people's feelings are the most popular members of any team. Drama projects can begin to teach these crucial skills effectively from a very young age.

Chapter 11

Ending on a high

Wherever your flights of fantasy and the children's imaginations have taken you during a drama class, you will need to bring everybody back together to end the session as a co-operative group again. You should aim to leave all of the children and the adults feeling exhilarated, but tired enough to be glad to calm down and move on to a different activity, while looking forward to their next drama session on another day.

CIRCLE TIME

Gather everybody together by enthusiastically announcing the last activities and putting yourself in the right place to begin. Depending on your group and on the previous activity, you may find that you need to call out and clap your hands, or you may achieve a more constructive response by whispering and beckoning to the children.

Action songs are usually the most successful way to end a session with this age group and a circle ensures that all the children feel equally valued and secure in the knowledge that they have their own place to sit or stand. Ending your session in this way each time indicates to the children in a very concrete way that the session is almost over and that soon they will be changing what they are doing. Some children, particularly very young ones, those who are still fairly new to a setting or shy within the group, and those with undeveloped communication skills or other special needs, rely on this kind of clue to the pattern of their day and are helped a great deal by the beginning and end of certain activities always being presented in the same way.

Some of the songs that you choose may require the children to hold hands at the beginning and some may need other positions. Peer group classes in school and nursery settings may enjoy ring games and holding hands with each other often. Many parents also find this is something that they can easily relate to and join in with when attending a private class. These games are very valuable for encouraging confidence and social skills, part of our children's heritage and also great fun.

However, since you are teaching drama, you could include some extracts from 'real' stage shows from the West End here, as well as or instead of a familiar ring game or action song. Many of the most popular and well-known shows contain a wealth of material that can be enjoyed by young children, along with the adults working with them. If you ask everybody to sit or stand in a circle and copy some very simple actions that you make up to fit the song, you can really end on a high!

Try to include holding hands within the circle at a particular point within the music and ensure that it goes on for long enough for all the children to have found the hands of the people either side of them if they wish to, as this demonstrates the togetherness of your group as a drama company. If a child refuses to hold hands with other children, they should not be forced to do so, but an adult may be able to sensitively hold one of their hands or include them within the sweep of their arm as they reach around to take the hand of the next child. Ensure that the extract you choose ends with a flourish and show children how to finish with their arms held high and a big smile on their face.

Figure 21 Teach children how to end the performance of a musical number with a flourish!

Other simple movements and actions that you could use include:

clapping hands (high and low, in front, to the sides and behind you);
stamping feet (while standing or sitting);
jumping or hopping;
snapping fingers;
clicking heels or knocking knees together;
swaying bodies;
swaying arms in the air;
spinning around;
tapping shoulders or knees or the floor;
pointing to everybody in the circle with a moving finger;
nodding or shaking heads;
beckoning with a whole hand;
'sunshine' arms overhead;
wiggling fingers;
standing up and sitting down;
or parts of the hand jive!

KEEP SOME FUN RIGHT TO THE END

Save one or two songs that the children really like, whether familiar or taught by you, to use at the end of your sessions. They should be quite tired by then and might need that encouragement to stay with the group right to the end. Rather than watching people drift off one by one and allowing the session to peter out in an anticlimatic way, you want everybody to come running to join in with the last activity because it is so much fun!

Not every session will be totally successful for all the children right to the end, but it is important to retain your enthusiasm for the song, the actions and the group until you have finished in the way you intended. Some children, and hopefully most of the adults, will have stayed with you and they will appreciate your stamina despite the distractions around. And, on another occasion, it will be different ones who manage everything. Sometimes, and more and more often as their dramatic experience grows, it will be everybody.

VALUE RELATIONSHIPS

You should aim to build constructive relationships with all of the children and their main caregivers or keyworkers. Value these relationships and the pleasure that they can give to you and to those you are working with. Drama is a very sociable activity, which can encourage people to get to know each other very quickly and to form friendships that might otherwise never have occurred.

Always thank all the children and adults, whether they are colleagues or the children's parents and other caregivers, at the end of a session and congratulate them for working hard. Tell them that you have enjoyed working with them and look forward to seeing them again next time and make sure that you mean what you are saying. If possible, allow for some relaxed time immediately after a class during which the adults may chat and exchange ideas and any concerns. Some parents or keyworkers will find it easier to talk with you after the drama session has 'warmed up' their confidence and your relationship.

If you are thanked in return, accept it gracefully and, if some of the children ask to kiss or hug you goodbye, enjoy the spontaneous way that they choose to show you how much they have enjoyed themselves. Children within the foundation stage like to express themselves with their whole bodies and this closeness is a natural extension of the work they share with you in drama. While you should never impose a kiss, hug or cuddle upon a child, it would not be right to refuse it if they want it within the relationship they are forming with you. They could interpret that as an indication that you don't really like them after all and feel hurt or confused. And, after all, stage people do hug each other all the time!

MOVING ON

Children continue to grow older and move on to new experiences throughout their lives. Sometimes at the end of each term and always at the end of each school year, you will find that some or all of the children in your classes will have to leave you. This can, at times, be sad because you will have become very fond of many of them and they may regard you with anything from mild liking to a form of hero worship.

It is important to express your feelings in a controlled and appropriate way and to allow the children to express theirs. Lead by example, saying that you will miss seeing them each week and that you will always remember how good they were at some of the dramatic activities. Allow them to express how they feel in whatever way they feel able to. Some may talk about their feelings, some may draw a picture or make a card for you, some may be upset while some may suddenly exhibit challenging or 'out of character' behaviour because they feel unable to cope with the impending changes in their lives.

Try to leave the children with a firm understanding that they will have their memories and the skills they have learned forever and that they will be able to use them in greater and greater projects as their lives continue. It is fun to look back, but important to look forward and to embrace new challenges with the strength gained from earlier ones.

If you do have an opportunity to see any of the children at any time in the future, once they are established in a later stage of their lives, always greet them with the pleasure that any of us feels when meeting with an old friend.

Whether or not you hold regular performances with the children in your groups or classes, it is always appropriate with young children to have some kind of a display towards the end of a school year. Parents, families and friends will be interested and pleased to have an opportunity to see what their children have been learning and they will wish to mark the 'leaving' and 'moving on' with a memorable event. This will also help the children to feel that their time and work with you achieved a satisfactory climax. And then – what a good excuse for a party!

Chapter 12

Performance skills

Most young children enjoy the opportunity to be the centre of attention, and even 'show off' a bit, when they feel secure within a situation and group of people. Offering them regular opportunities to stand onstage and speak, act, mime, sing or dance allows them to discover, develop and display their natural expressive abilities and enjoy sharing them with an audience. This builds a degree of self-confidence that will prove valuable in many varied situations throughout their lives.

USING A STAGE

If you are lucky enough to have a stage, or blocks that can be built into a stage, you will be able to encourage the children to enjoy performing to an audience while standing onstage. Introduce the concept of the stage carefully. Many children may be fascinated by it, but some may be nervous or a little afraid of standing on a raised floor surface with others looking at them.

Begin by climbing onto the stage and standing there yourself, while the children remain on the floor level. Ask them if they can see you and why they can now all see you more easily than when you were all on the floor together. Explain that performers stand onstage to allow their audience to see them clearly. Invite them all to join you onstage and stand there, together with you. Then step down yourself and exclaim from the floor how well you can now see them.

Take all safety aspects into careful consideration. If there are steps up to the stage, make sure that all children can climb them easily. If any of the children are very small or have special physical needs, assist them sensitively by offering them a hand or arm to grasp as they step up, so that they may let go as soon as they feel safe and it is not made obvious that they need more help than others in the group. If a child is wary of the steps or standing onstage, allow them to walk up and stand beside you or another child who is happy to be sensitively helpful. If all of the children are small but daring, insist that they all accept a guiding hand when moving up onto or down from the stage, to avoid any tripping and falling accidents!

Do not force a child who is genuinely worried or upset by the idea of standing onstage, but allow them to watch the others a few times and then gradually encourage small progressions, such as climbing up and then immediately stepping down again, then standing onstage with you or another child but just watching and listening, then speaking, singing or dancing within a group of friends, before attempting to do anything alone.

Explain to all the children that they must never stand too close to the front of a stage, as it is easy to accidentally step off and it may be a long way down. Always stand close to the front of a stage, and ask any assisting adults to do so too, to remind children when their feet are too close to the edge and to catch a child if they do take a step too far!

If the floor surface in front of the stage is very hard, you could place a gymnastic mat, floor cushions or a soft rug there to break a fall, just in case. Look for markings on the stage or mark out a line with chalk or coloured sticky tape and impress upon children that they should always stay behind the line.

A DESIGNATED STAGE AREA

If you do not have access to a stage of any kind, you could mark out a special area on the floor to use. Depending on the floor surface, and whether you have to remove it after each session, use chalk, coloured sticky tape, gymnastic mats or a piece of carpet. Introduce the area to the children as a special place to be, always refer to it as 'the stage' and treat it in the same way as a raised stage. However, you would not need to worry about the safety aspects in the same way, as children would be able to access it easily from the floor and would not come to harm if they 'fell off'.

THE RIGHT WORDS

Young children absorb language rapidly and love long and special words. They always want to know the names of everything and remember unusual ones just as easily as more common ones, if they are introduced in a meaningful context and used regularly within activities and instructions that they can understand. There is no reason at all not to use the correct names for parts of the stage, items used in stagework and people who work in the theatre. Teach any of them through the playing of games and then include them naturally in conversation and when explaining what you would like the children to do.

Here are the most useful ones to help you, in case you were not stage trained yourself!

DIRECTIONS

Upstage	Away from the audience, towards the back of the stage.
Downstage	Close to the audience, towards the front of the stage.
Stage left	The side at your left hand when you are standing onstage, facing the audience.
Stage right	The side at your right hand when you are standing onstage, facing the audience.
Stage centre	In the middle of the stage.

These terms can be combined to give instructions or play movement games. For example:

> Stand at downstage centre, then move upstage and face stage right. The group at upstage left moves to downstage right, then the group at downstage left moves to upstage centre.

You will notice that the terms *stage left* and *stage right* are very important. A group of people within a cast who are asked to move merely to right or left may interpret that to mean different things, which could be disastrous in a dance routine! The audience's left and right are opposite to the performers' left and right , unless the performers have their back to the audience. Of course, there are times within a dance or mime sequence when they may turn their backs, but usually they will be required to face front. Therefore, everybody needs to remember that *stage left* and *stage right* refer to performers' directions when standing onstage and facing the audience.

It is correct to say *onstage* and *offstage,* without the addition of the word 'the' in the middle. Children can be invited to *enter* and *exit*, as well as 'come on' and 'go off'.

NAMES AND PLACES

Wing	The area at the side of the stage where performers may wait and through which they enter and exit. These are described as the *stage left wing* and the *stage right wing.*
Green room	A room or extended wing area in which performers wait to go onstage. (It does not have to be painted green!)
Greys	The curtains at the back of the stage, which, in a real theatre, are grey or silvery in colour, to prevent unwanted shadows caused by reflected light.
Backrun	The passage behind the greys through which performers and backstage crew can walk to pass between one wing and the other, unseen by the audience.
Housetabs	The main curtains that cover the stage before and after a performance and can be pulled for scene changes.
Auditorium	The place where the audience sits to watch a performance.
Front of house	All the areas used by the audience and not by the performers – auditorium, refreshment and waiting rooms, etc.

House lights	The main lights within the auditorium and other public areas.
Stage lights	The spotlights that are trained on the performers and light up the stage.

House lights and stage lights do not come on together. The house lights are turned off by the front of house team before the stage lights are turned on, and are turned on again after the stage lights are off. The correct stage terms are lights up and lights down.

Backdrop	A relevant picture painted on or created from fabric and hung or pinned to the greys behind the actors as a display to set the scene.
Set	Pieces of free-standing scenery carried on and offstage when needed.
Props	Objects used onstage to add to the story or develop the characters. Short for 'properties'.
Costume	Clothes worn to create characters or effects onstage.
Script	Book or sheet of words and directions that everyone on and behind stage follows and adheres to. The correct name is 'Libretto'.
Score	Book or sheets containing music and song words for musicians and singers to follow.
Lyrics	Song words.
Lines	Words said onstage – can be learned from a script or improvised around an agreed idea or storyline.
Cue	The word or action that occurs immediately before a performer's part, indicating that it is now his or her turn.
Prompt	A reminder of a line or what to do next, given by someone following a script in a wing.
Act	Part of a show between the beginning or end and an interval – usually two in a performance, sometimes three.

Scene	A section of a show after which there is a change in characters, storyline or setting.
Musical number	A song and/or dance routine performed as an integral part of a show.

PEOPLE

Producer	In overall charge of a production, taking care of all the tasks that have to be completed, from hiring of venues and staff to organising of tickets and refreshments.
Director	Arranges rehearsal schedules, plans and leads rehearsals, helps those onstage to perform to the best of their abilities and liases with backstage crews and lighting technicians to ensure the smooth running of the show. In smaller and amateur companies, one person often takes on both of these roles, but it is a huge amount of work and responsibility.
Choreog-rapher	Plans, sets, demonstrates and teaches dances and movement sequences.
Musical director	Arranges, teaches and plays or conducts music for songs and instrumental sequences.
Cast	Everybody who performs onstage during the course of a production.
Technician	In charge of setting up technical equipment and making it work appropriately throughout performances. Lighting technicians and sound technicians may work separately, or one person or team may arrange both.
Backstage crew	In charge of sets, props, housetabs and any special effects throughout performances.
Front of house team	Responsible for the safety of the audience. They may sell programmes and refreshments, monitor audience behaviour and evacuate the building in case of fire.

ADAPT TO THE NEEDS OF YOUR GROUP

Obviously, no foundation stage child needs to learn all of these names, but many of them will enjoy learning a few and it is best to use whichever seem most appropriate to the work you are doing. You may use some in one term and different ones in the following term, returning to a few old ones and adding new ones the next year. Since everything needs a name or a label to ensure that everybody knows what is being discussed, it makes sense to use correct ones from the beginning to avoid later confusions or having to learn everything twice.

SPEAKING ONSTAGE

Children can learn to chant in unison to give them the encouragement and confidence that they need to speak onstage. This can make a good introduction to a performance. For example:

> Hello everybody and welcome to our show! (or the name of your class or setting)
> We are the little pigs!
> Teddies love Christmas!
> Monkeys live in the jungle!

Figure 22 Children speaking or chanting in unison can make a good introduction to a performance.

Encourage the children to remember the skills they have acquired and practised in enunciation and voice projection, and to speak loudly and clearly without shouting. Ask them to maintain a sensible speed and not to slow down further and further while waiting for each other to come in. There is nothing worse for an audience than having to listen to a group of children groaning and grumbling along together at the rate of one word a minute! Praising a child who is a good leader for their confident speech and correct speed usually ensures that they will work hard to maintain it and that others will follow them, rather than the other way around. Impress upon the children that it is not wrong to be the one who is heard by the audience to be confidently leading the others – at this age it never can be!

Wherever possible, allow children opportunities to speak individually onstage from the youngest age. They are then unlikely to develop any real shyness or self-consciousness about it later in life (even if they feel that they must occasionally pretend some at certain stages and in certain situations to fit in with their peer group).

If there are only a few children, saying their names and ages, or ideas on a theme, in turn can be enchanting for an audience of families and friends to watch and listen to. If they retain their natural spontaneity and say something amusing, be proud of their confidence and allow the audience to enjoy the joke in a sensitive manner. Very young children usually enjoy laughter around them and will just join in when they hear it. If you have a large group of children, you could arrange for them to speak in small groups, or, if you perform regularly, offer just the oldest children opportunities to speak individually, so that each child understands that they will have their turn when they are the oldest in the group.

If a child is suddenly reluctant to speak, even if they are usually the most talkative of all, just prompt them or speak for them and move on without fuss. There will always be some surprises in performance. The boldest child may be overwhelmed and the quietest may have been saving it all for the big occasion!

Children who are afraid to speak onstage or into a microphone at all at the age of 2 or 3, but who learn, practise and experience drama regularly, may soon be competing with each other in a friendly way to give the best speech. Within a year, children may take part in two or three successful performances and a couple of inaudible whispered names onstage may give way to such polished comedy routines as 'My name's Charlotte and I'm twenty-nine!'; 'And my name's Katie and I'm forty-three-and-a-half!'

A SIMPLE PERFORMANCE

The most successful children's performances usually rely on action songs, dances and mime sequences and acted stories set to music.

If several children are singing, dancing or acting together, each part will be remembered by somebody and they will happily copy each other and work together to achieve the whole scene or musical number. It may also be entertaining for an audience to watch the children playing a short game of musical statues onstage, because they love to freeze in interesting shapes and usually concentrate hard and then giggle!

Remind the children that the audience would like to see their faces, so they should try to remember always to face front when they are singing or speaking. Encourage them to smile all the time, except when they are making another expression in an acted sequence, and to sing along to as much of each song and piece of music as they know. Ensure that the children have had lots of opportunities to practise everything that they will perform and that they feel confident of what to do. This means putting songs, sequences and speeches into an appropriate order and practising them in this order for some days or weeks before the performance. Children always like to know what will come next and will only be confident if they are sure of which song or activity will follow which one, what the music will sound like and where they will be standing or sitting at the beginning and end of each number.

IN A NURSERY OR SCHOOL SETTING

You will probably be asked to arrange for the children in your class or group to perform at least once a year, as part of a Christmas entertainment or an end of year celebration in the summer. There may also be other special events which your setting participates in.

Sometimes a class or group will provide their own performance separately; sometimes they will form a part of the whole entertainment in conjunction with the rest of the school or nursery. If you are not totally responsible for the entire performance, make sure that you spend lots of time talking with other staff and planning and agreeing in advance who will be responsible for what and where each class or group will fit in. If you have any particular needs for your performance, such as set pieces or props or extra facilities to accommodate children with special needs, decide in advance how you will provide them with the minimum of fuss and practise this before the big day.

Staff members will obviously all be present for a performance in their setting and will have made time to practise and rehearse with all the children in the preceding days and weeks. You may decide that it is best for one or more staff members to perform with the children or to be onstage with them to offer moral support and ensure safety. Or, staff may feel that the children are able to perform alone, but choose to sit behind or to the sides of the stage or in the wings or backrun to help them on and offstage and to be close enough to help if needed. The children should be able to see their familiar teachers and keyworkers easily from the stage if they need to. Encouraging smiles are all that most of them will need to give their best and enjoy themselves in performing.

IN PRIVATE CLASSES

If you run weekly classes for children privately, you do not have to arrange for performances. But, since drama is essentially a performing art, it is a rewarding thing to do and many parents may request or expect a number of opportunities to watch their children onstage.

We all work harder and with more enthusiasm if we know that we are working towards an end product that we can be proud of. Try to arrange for a performance at least once a year. If possible, arrange for one at the end of each term, because many clients may not stay with the class for a whole year, so some children could miss out on this valuable opportunity. Children in the foundation stage mature, develop and change so quickly that they can make enormous progress within ten to twelve weeks and there is no easier or pleasanter way of displaying this to parents than to invite them to watch their children perform.

You may choose to perform onstage with the children, especially if you are bringing together more than one class who do not all know each other well, or if you are including some very young children, some newer, shyer or less confident ones or any with special needs. This can be a valuable opportunity to display your own skills to the children's families and to let them see the good relationship that you have with each child, as you share in their excitement and support them to achieve everything you have planned and practised. However, you must be sure of your own ability to concentrate and motivate the children throughout the performance and enjoy the experience yourself. You may have to carry on despite a strong desire to laugh, as children are marvellously unpredictable and will always surprise us! (The hardest act I ever had to follow was when we were performing a mime about putting a horse into its stable and one of my most adorable 4-year-olds suddenly announced clearly to the audience, 'My horse is going to have her baby now – would you like to watch?')

If you think that all of the children will be happy to perform without you beside them, you could consider standing behind the audience and offering encouragement and reminders from there. But do ensure that you are not a distraction to the audience or irritating to the children! You will need to ask a colleague to operate sound equipment and house tabs for you. Make sure that you discuss and rehearse the performance with them before the children arrive!

You might wish to sit close to the stage, just in case a child suddenly needs help or is unhappy and needs to be removed from the stage. If you are onstage performing yourself, ensure that a colleague or trusted parent or nanny is seated close to the stage area and ready to help a child to leave the stage if necessary. Children of this age should not be expected to 'get it all right', but they should not be left onstage in performance if they are disrupting or upsetting the other children, or if they are unhappy or likely to try to climb down on their own. It is possible to quickly and sensitively remove a child and return them to a parent or carer or take them to sit with another staff member without upsetting anyone else. You should discuss this eventuality with the children's families and caregivers in advance and ensure that they understand that this is the way their child would be handled.

Depending on the clients in your groups or classes, you may decide that it would be best to make the last class of a term a performance followed by a party. Or you may decide to offer a separate performance session and make attendance optional. This will depend on whether you feel that extended family members would like to attend and would find it easier at a weekend, or whether it would be better for your group to keep the audience small and invite only the caregivers who usually attend classes.

You may have a group of children whose ages and abilities are very mixed and some may be very ready to perform while others are not. In this case, you may need to keep the performance separate and advise parents and carers carefully on whether they should consider attending to participate, attending to watch or waiting until their child is older or more confident. Or you may have a peer group class of children who should all have the opportunity to participate and therefore you might need to stick to the day and time of their usual session, in case any families are not free to give up extra time at the weekend or whenever you choose.

If you do offer a separate performance session, you will need to consider whether you should arrange for refreshments on that day and how to arrange seating and limit audience numbers to adhere to required safety guidelines. You will also have to arrange for the extra hire of your venue and any colleagues that you may like to ask for help on the day, so you may need to ask parents to contribute towards this through the payment of a small 'performance fee'. Only those children who participate will pay the fee.

Be aware that, if you sell or make a charge for your tickets, you must take out more complicated short term public liability insurance, but, if the tickets are free or only donations are asked for, you do not need to do this. Most groups and settings would find it difficult to charge enough for their tickets to cover the insurance costs, whether advertising to the public or just an invited audience, and will perform to a much larger and more sympathetic and appreciative audience if they are only required to make a donation or purchase programmes and refreshments.

You will need to impress upon parents that they must make a decision in advance about whether their children are ready and keen to take part, let you know their decision and then stick to it. Offer as much tactful advice as is requested, or as you feel is necessary, but make sure that it is the child's main caregiver who makes the final decision. They know their own child best and the occasion is only likely to be a success if they are fully supportive. It is, of course, impossible to gain absolute reliability from such young children and their busy families. You may still find that one or two children fail to turn up after all, because they are unwell or their car breaks down, but the majority of your group should be secure. Avoid relying on any one child to say a particular line or lead a particular song or movement, but rather rehearse two or three in each role, or one or two from each class if several are coming together, to perform together or cover for each other. If a child suddenly refuses to go onstage on the day, just allow them to watch with their family in the audience.

If your performance is separate, you will need to make the last session of the term special for all the children in another way. The best way is often to hold your performance at the weekend just before the week of your last classes and to invite all class members to participate in the 'after-show and end-of-term party' at their usual session time during the last week of your term. Make it very clear to parents, carers and children that everybody is welcome at the party, whether they performed or not, and allow them all to share in dressing up in costumes, playing instruments, party and ring games and refreshments in a relaxed and happy atmosphere.

COSTUMES

A group of small children dressed similarly in attractive outfits make a performance look worthwhile before it even begins and most young children love to dress up in special costumes. It is worthwhile to design and use costumes in any performance, but they do need to be simple to obtain and assemble, and comfortable to wear.

Plain clothes, appropriate to the season, in colours that symbolise the animal or character being acted are an excellent base and can usually be supplied by the children themselves. For example:

white jumpers and tights for rabbits in winter;
pink or black T-shirts and shorts for pigs in summer;
blue sweatshirts, red trousers and wellington boots for winter soldiers;
frilly dresses with wings and hairbands for summer fairies;
long T-shirts tied with a sash or belt over shorts and 'dwarf' hats made from card or fabric for summer pixies or elves.

In summer, the children can go barefoot if the floor surface of your stage area is safe from splinters and other hazards. If you are uncertain, lay down a non-slip mat or carpet for them to stand on or ask them to wear plimsolls, ballet shoes, canvas shoes or sandals in keeping with their costume. In winter, they can wear just socks or tights if the floor surface is safe and not slippery, or wear an appropriate type of shoe or boot.

To add the finishing touches to a costume you can make ears or headdresses attached to headbands made of paper or card or to children's plastic hairbands. Tails can be made from card or fabric and attached to the back of the children's costumes with a safety pin. This is quite safe, so long as all children are carefully supervised while wearing the tails and they are removed by adults as soon as the performance is over. If at all possible, involve the children in making hats, ears and headdresses for themselves, with as much help and support as necessary, and allow them to take them home or keep them to play with in their nursery or classroom after the show.

Thoroughly test any new ideas and costumes before going ahead with them in a performance situation! Children can become very upset and unable to perform if they are worried that their headdress will fall off if they move, or if they are asked to wear a mask without opportunities to practise wearing it in advance. Allow children to wear costume items in rehearsal or during free play periods to get used to them. It is important not to send all costume items home with children in advance unless you are sure that they will all remember to bring them back on the day, but it may help one or two reluctant children to participate if they have been able to take them and practise wearing them with their familiar carers.

You may encounter some families who feel that their child cannot perform just because they are unable to provide the necessary costume items. You will need to explain to them that the decision should be based on their child's needs, not whether they can afford to buy a pink T-shirt or a pair of plimsolls, and make it clear that you will arrange to lend costume items to any child who doesn't have them. If you have children of your own, you will probably have plenty of spare and outgrown clothes in all colours. If not, you will have friends and colleagues who do, or you could ask other parents to lend any spares that they have.

Discuss individual children's and families' needs and preferences in a relaxed way well in advance and offer help as required. And always have spares of everything with you at the performance venue!

REMEMBER THE BOWS

Spend some time from the beginning of drama work teaching children to take a bow. Some may say that they prefer to curtsey, especially if they attend dance classes, and reassure them that that is also fine. Make no distinctions with this age group as to who should bow and who should curtsey. Although is is unusual for men to curtsey, boys should have the opportunity to try it while they are still young and exploring if they choose to. Women bow, as well as curtsey, throughout their lives, so girls should always have a free choice.

Begin with simple bows from the waist and move on to more elaborate ideas. Suggest that children find their own new and different ways of taking bows. They may put their arms across their bodies or behind their backs, or sweep an arm before them with a twirling hand. They may hold hands in a line or stand separately in their own spaces. Have fun exploring ways to bow. Explain to the children that taking a bow means 'I've finished. Thank you for watching.'

Figure 23 Taking a bow means 'I've finished. Thank you for watching.'

Teach them to accept and enjoy applause. They should always be proud of their achievements onstage and understand that it is always nice to hear that an audience has appreciated your efforts enough to feel that they would like to clap.

Certificates and stickers are increasingly popular as rewards for this age group and they are fairly cheap and easy to buy or make in any quantity. It is often much appreciated by parents and children if you are able to provide these at the end of a performance or an end of term party. Whether you do this or not, make sure that you give the children lots of praise for their efforts and remember to thank them and their families for their support and commitment throughout the rehearsal and performance period.

A warm thank you and an offer of friendship within a professional relationship costs nothing, but gains a great deal – including the goodwill of clients who will stay for the following term and the next show and go on to recommend you, your classes or your setting to all their friends!

Chapter 13

Going it alone

If reading this book, or trying out the ideas in a setting, has inspired you to want to devote more of your time to sharing drama with children, their families and their caregivers, you may like to consider setting up private classes or offering regular sessions to a number of establishments with foundation stage children.

An experienced and confident practitioner can use the ideas and activities described within this book to plan a programme of classes which may be offered to groups of children privately (for example, weekly classes in a village hall), or to nurseries and pre-schools on a peripatetic basis. In these situations, it is important to work in partnership with parents, nannies and other home-based carers in private classes or with key workers in each setting.

The youngest children and those with special needs may require additional adult support on a one-to-one or one-to-two ratio, to enable them to participate fully in sessions. All children benefit from their parents or carers being involved enough to discuss the drama activities with them between sessions and to help them to remember the characters and songs that they have enjoyed. Parents and carers or fellow practitioners should also be made to feel welcome and included in the session as adults in their own right, as well as nurturers of the children. Encourage them to share confidences with you before you chat with the children whenever they feel that this would help.

IN A NURSERY OR SCHOOL SETTING

A practitioner entering any number of nursery, pre-school or school settings must develop and maintain a healthy relationship with members of staff within each setting. It may be helpful to think of yourself as a 'breath of fresh air' entering from outside, bringing new experiences to enhance the provision already offered. But you must be careful to fit in as much as possible with the routine and structure that the children are used to.

BEFORE EACH SESSION

Arrive in good time to set up equipment and prepare your space, but not too early, as that space may still be in use until just before the drama session. The first time you visit a setting you will need a practitioner to show and explain everything to you. Assess the working space and ask any questions and mention any possible concerns or potential difficulties then.

After the first time, you should expect to be able to use the same room or area for each session and to prepare without needing the help or supervision of other staff, who have their own work to do. But be flexible!

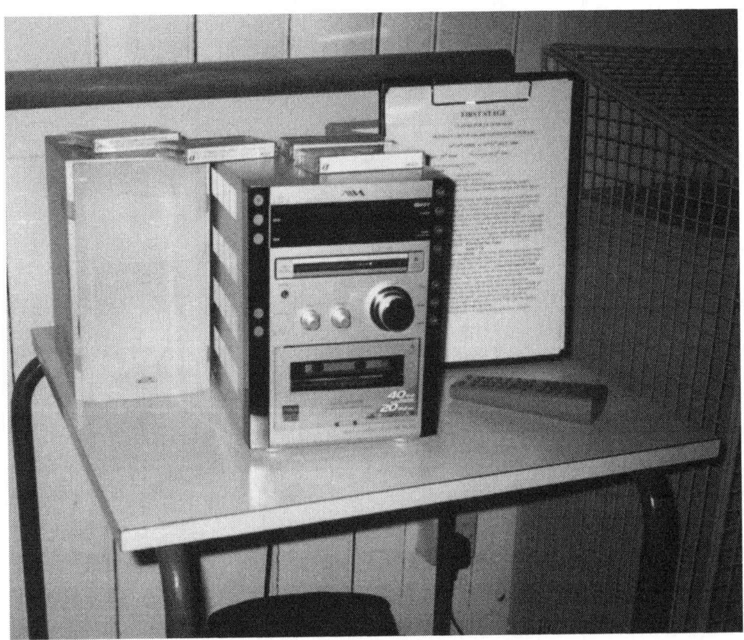

Figure 24 A reliable tape player and your own carefully prepared tapes are the most essential pieces of equipment.

If an accident has occurred or a special project is in progress, it will not harm anybody to occasionally work on drama in a different room. You should aim to provide all your own equipment that travels with you, but, if there is anything you need to borrow (such as a tape player on the day yours has broken), you should aim to let the setting know in advance and check that they will be able to provide it.

MAKING RELATIONSHIPS

Ensure that you give the full length of time promised to the session each time you visit the setting and stick to the times agreed. Ask for a written list of the children's first names and ages for each group that you will be working with and details of any special needs or circumstances that you need to be aware of. Study these and learn them by heart as quickly as possible. You cannot lead a group until you are fully confident of each child's name and some names may be unusual, from another culture or differently spelt or pronounced.

While each child will, of course, have an individual level of ability and confidence, each month of a child's age can make a tremendous difference to them and you should not be surprised or confused when a tall, well-grown 3-year-old or a small, delicate 5-year-old displays age appropriate maturity because you had only their appearance to assist your expectations.

IN PRIVATE CLASSES

You are responsible for hiring your own venue and checking it for safety, cleanliness and suitability for your use. Space and floor surface are important, as is access to toilets for the children. If possible, hire a smaller venue, such as a village hall, which will allow you to hold your own key and be the sole user during your sessions. Shared facilities, such as community centres, have an open front door and more than one group using the building at the same time, which can mean sharing toilet facilities with unknown adults, and clients may feel less confident about leaving their child with you.

BEFORE EACH SESSION

It is your duty to make the venue look attractive and welcoming and to arrive in time to turn on heaters or fans to ensure a comfortable temperature before clients come in. Set up your equipment and be ready in good time for clients arriving, so that you have time to chat with them or answer queries.

All equipment must be your own and easily transportable, as you must set it up and remove it for each session, without having to pay for long periods of hall hire just for this purpose. Prepare as much as possible at home, leaving only furniture to move and bags to be opened on arrival. Pack things back into their appropriate bags and take them home after the children leave.

You will need a tape and/or CD player and the tapes or CDs that you intend to use (with copies or back-ups in case of accidents), a bag of any other props that you intend to bring out later in the session, your attendance register (which must be marked before the session begins and updated if a child arrives later, in case there should be a fire in the building and a need to take everybody outside), payment records, information sheets with registration forms and any letters that you wish to give out to clients, a first aid kit suitable for children, a mobile telephone and your cash box. It is also sensible to have tissues and wet wipes, pens and scrap paper available for anybody to use.

Figure 25 If you are running a private class in hired accommodation you will need to be very organised in preparing and transporting your equipment to and from the venue.

Put everything out of the way on small tables at the sides of the room, but avoid putting out any chairs (though have some available for a pregnant mother or watching grandfather) to ensure that there is space and encouragement for everybody to join in. Also, keep the space as bare and undistracting as possible. Few young children are able to concentrate on a drama session in the middle of a room, if the walls around them are lined with shelves of toys or books!

Your lesson plan notes are easiest to use if they are on a clipboard and kept near to you for easy referral. A remote control for your player prevents you having to leave the circle of children or rush through the group of dancers or actors to turn music on or off.

MAKING RELATIONSHIPS

A selection of children's books, which changes each week, made available on the floor before a session ensures that clients are prepared to arrive in time, knowing that they will have something to do with their child and will not feel embarrassed to stand around waiting or struggle to control their child who sees a large empty space and wants to run around. A calm moment spent reading a story or looking at a book can put children into a focused frame of mind from which they will be receptive to a drama session, while running around in a hall is likely to over-excite or tire them and lead to accidents and upsets before the session begins.

Providing photograph albums from previous terms – photographs of the children taken in classes, performances and parties with parents' permission – can be a wonderful talking point between clients and children. Older members of the class grow in self-esteem by seeing themselves in your 'special book' and can be asked to find themselves and their friends and explain what was going on in the pictures to newer members, whose ambition then becomes to have their photograph in your book too!

Remember always to ask for permission before taking photographs of children and provide a simple way for parents to refuse if they need to. They could talk privately to you or to any staff member, or write their name on a list that you have provided. In this way, they will not feel embarrassed to withhold their permission and can feel confident that they will not be asked to explain their reasons before other parents.

Verbal permission is usually enough if the photographs will stay in albums in your possession and only be shown to class members. Written permission is needed for any photographs to be used in a book or publicity brochure or leaflet that may be sold or distributed to the public. You will need to provide a form that parents can sign to give this permission, detailing the purposes of the pictures and their likely distribution.

It is possible to sensitively exclude young children from photographs without their knowledge if necessary, to avoid them becoming upset or feeling unwanted. You could point the camera in their direction too, but never press the button, or take pictures when they are at the far side of a group and just outside the frame, or take pictures but then erase them from a digital camera, or give all of the pictures to the child's parent.

Children's names should never appear with their photographs without a good reason, and at the express written permission of the child's parents or guardians.

Looking at photographs can be an excellent opportunity for you to chat informally with children in a friendly way. You may find out that the shy child who is not yet able to answer any questions within the group actually has extremely well-developed language skills and mature understanding and the child who appeared to be paying little attention last week remembers every song and character mentioned.

It is important to start on time, being flexible by two or three minutes. If a child is just taking off their coat or using the toilet, it is courteous to wait for them to join the group. If a client has requested your advice or indicated their need to give you some information about their child, it is not appropriate to end the conversation by looking at the clock, unless you feel that more than a minute or two will be required and you can offer to talk after the session instead.

If clients see that you never start on time because you wait for those who are regularly late, they will all begin to arrive later and later and sessions will run into difficulties. But, it is important to let clients know that, if they are sometimes late, they are still able to join in at whichever point you have reached and to make the child feel that they are always welcome.

Since parents are paying for a whole session, you must ensure that they have the time you promised. But, if they have a commitment immediately after the class, such as collecting another child from school, they will find it worrying to attend if you run late and do not finish within five minutes of the time agreed. Clients do not continue with a class in the long term if they find fitting it into their schedule too stressful.

It is very important to indicate clearly to everybody that the session is about to officially begin. Announce that it is 'time to get on' or 'time to get started' in a loud, confident and enthusiastic voice and immediately enlist the children's help in putting away the books into a bag or box, warning the adults in a friendly way that 'chatting time' is about to come to an end if they are going to join in, or that it is time to say goodbye to their child(ren) if they are going into another room or leaving the premises. Give special attention at this time to any children attending without a familiar adult and any who benefit from extra support. Some will be perfectly happy to sit with their friends and classmates and expectantly wait for the first activity; others may feel a little wobbly until they have sung the first song. Experienced practitioners will be able to use their professional judgement to decide on the best way to encourage each child.

As long as you can meet the correct adult to child ratio, you can offer parents and carers the choice of joining in with their children, watching them, going into another room if one is available, or leaving them with you and returning at the end of the session. Many adults, particularly nannies and childminders, may always choose to participate because they enjoy sharing drama with the children too. Others may be glad to gradually increase their child's independence by withdrawing to watch, but being close by if their child needs extra support in certain activities.

Those with babies and toddlers may like to sit in another room to play with them and chat to each other, while those with confident older children may appreciate the opportunity to go home or go shopping for a short while, knowing that their child is engaged in a worthwhile activity. In this case, you must ensure that you have a contact telephone number, to use if the child should be hurt, unwell or unhappy or if they are delayed and do not return by the end of the session to collect the child.

In a private class, children will arrive individually and from a wide range of situations and experiences. They may also be accompanied by a variety of different adults.

It is a good idea to get to know parents' names and to use them, as adults don't really feel comfortable calling each other 'Mrs Brown' or 'Sophie's Mummy' once they have known each other for a while. The simplest way to memorise parents' names is to read through the children's registration forms regularly and to take notice when parents speak to or about each other. If a grandparent brings a child, you must ask what the child calls them, as a child who is asked to stand beside 'Grandma' will not understand what to do if they have come with 'Nana'! Nannies and childminders are usually called by their first names by their charges and all adults within the group will soon get used to this. I always find it best to ask everybody to use my first name only, for everything but cheques!

It may be appropriate to mention some very special news to the group before beginning – such as a child's birthday on that very day or a new baby sibling born since the last time you saw a child – but discourage children from expecting to think up a tale about a very minor event with which to regale the entire group every week, as this wastes too much precious learning time and causes fidgeting and loss of focus at the wrong time. If you make it clear to children that you would like to talk to them and hear what they have to say after the drama session, and take care to remember and listen as promised, they will usually be happy to wait. This is an excellent opportunity for them to learn how and when to make appropriate conversation and to practise temporary postponement of gratification.

In a private class, it is a good idea to make sure that any parents or carers who stay for the sessions are aware of the difference between 'sibling tiffs' and real disagreements. Brothers and sisters, cousins, next-door neighbours and close friends attending a class together may be more competitive or have more of a tendency to argue with each other than others in the class. It is important to discuss the children's relationships with their parents or caregivers (out of the children's hearing) and to agree on the most effective method of dealing with any rivalry that might occur. What matters most is that the influential adults in the children's lives are consistent in the areas of discipline and expectations of behaviour.

Parents and nannies who have only one child (or one child and a small baby) may have had no experience at all yet of normal life with two or more children growing up together and may incorrectly judge sibling behaviour as 'naughty' or 'disruptive'. Some well-timed explanations and careful exposure to other families in a relaxed situation may prove to be an ideal learning experience for them and prepare them for what may be to come in their lives!

It is important to greet all children, younger siblings and accompanying adults as they walk through the door and indicate that you are pleased to see them all. Suitable opening comments might be:

> We're so pleased to see you, Eleanor, because you're so good at singing.
>
> Toby was hoping you'd be here today, Thomas, because you were such good friends last week.
>
> I saw your Daddy yesterday, Daisy, and he told me how much you were looking forward to coming to drama today.

> I remember how good you are at being a bear, George, and I thought we might do some more work on bears today.

If a child arrives late, help them to integrate immediately with a statement such as:

> Come and join us, Alfie! You're just in time for our listening game!
> We must have sung so beautifully that Callahan heard us and came quickly to join in!

COSTS, BUDGETS, INVOICING AND ACCEPTING PAYMENT

If you are employed within an establishment or by an authority to work in various settings of their choice, you will receive an agreed salary for the job you do and not need to deal with money. But, if you make private arrangements to travel to settings or run private classes in one or more venues of your choosing, you must handle payments yourself. This is often a drama teacher's least favourite part of the job, but it is crucial unless you want to become a voluntary worker!

IN A NURSERY OR SCHOOL SETTING

Be aware that nurseries, pre-schools and schools have budgets and cannot always have exactly what they would like, even if it would be ideal for the children. If a setting has not much money to spare for extras, the children will still benefit from a very short drama session each week or a session once a fortnight or even once a month.

It may be possible to accommodate a large group of children working together, in order to keep costs down, if enough staff and space are available. Or it may work well to divide children into groups who take turns to participate in a weekly drama session at their setting.

Some settings may feel that it would be appropriate to ask parents to contribute a very small extra sum each week or month to allow their children to participate in drama. In this case, you should ensure that the setting assumes the responsibility for collecting the money and that you are not informed of which families have paid or not paid. No child should ever be excluded from participating because of non-payment by their family.

Settings with money to spend may have clear ideas of how many sessions they would like and which children should attend together, or staff may like to discuss or try out a range of options with you until you find the 'best fit' that suits everybody. Agree on a regular payment date with each setting and give them invoices in advance. Some settings prefer to pay for everything weekly, some monthly and some half-termly or termly. Any of these options can work, so long as you both know and keep clear records of exactly how much is owed and how and when it should be paid. It is sensible to offer a trial first session, which is paid for in advance or on the day, and then to enter into an agreement if both you and the setting wish to continue to work together regularly.

Occasionally, you may become involved with a setting that simply does not pay its bills. There may be a range of excuses – a member of staff is sick, someone forgot to collect the money from parents, the invoice or cheque has been lost, the chequebook is unexpectedly empty, the cheque is in the post (and never arrives), the bank must have made a mistake, etc. Do not accept any excuses. Simply issue another invoice with the payment due date written on it and state how long you are prepared to wait for the money. If you think there may be a genuine reason, you could allow up to a week. If not, or if it seems unlikely that the setting can pay its bills anymore, you will need to put in writing that you cannot offer any more sessions until the outstanding invoice has been paid.

When you do finally get the payment, you will need to decide whether this is likely to happen again. It is too uncomfortable and frustrating to go on working in a situation where you are unsure of being paid. Your work, enthusiasm and commitment inevitably suffer!

IN PRIVATE CLASSES

You must set the fees for classes that you set up and run privately. Finding the right level of fees is a delicate balancing act. It is helpful to do some research into how much other groups and individuals charge for extra-curricular activities for the same age range in your area. You must then take into account how many staff they employ, what type of equipment they use and the kind of venue they take place in.

It may seem tempting to simply 'undercut' other providers to attract new clients at first, but, if fees are too low to meet costs and provide you with a working wage, you will quickly resent the amount of time and care that you put into your preparation and leading of classes and may seek to raise fees too soon or cut corners.

Clients will also do their research and, if your classes are much cheaper than others, some people will think that they are probably not worthwhile (since one usually gets what one pays for). Others will come along only because you are the cheapest option and not because they have any interest in their children learning drama. If few of the children and their parents or carers have any real desire to work on drama skills, the class will not 'take off' and you may quickly lose those who were hoping for a good experience. This can cause your classes to fold or everyone to become disillusioned with your original ideas.

You should aim to keep fees at the same level for as long as possible, as most clients get used to paying particular sums regularly and only notice the increases. If you operate in term-times only, you will find that total amounts vary with the length of each term anyway. It is a good idea to offer parents a choice of payment options – e.g. termly, half-termly and monthly (and even weekly for a few families who would otherwise be unable to attend). But you must keep a clear and visible record of payments that can be easily shared with parents. A separate page in the attendance register is often a good place to record these details, but ensure that families' debts are not displayed for other clients to see and comment upon.

Clients appreciate being able to pay separately for the first week they attend and then take home the necessary written information and registration forms to return with further payment if they choose to continue with the classes. This gives them time to come to an informed decision that they are then likely to stick to. It also avoids free trial classes being taken by clients who never intend to make a regular commitment.

The majority of parents and carers will get used to where they can look to check the fees they should pay, whether this is in the register, a notice on display or on a letter which you hand out to them, and know that they should make payments at the beginning of each term or half-term. Others may be happy to ask regularly how much they owe and when they need to pay. If you have a standard slip of paper for outstanding fees which you can fill in with a name and amount and hand out whenever a client does forget to pay, you can keep the money separate from the service and the people involved and avoid embarrassment on both sides.

Many parents are so used to paying various fees for classes and activities for themselves and their children now that the only thing they make a note of is to remember to bring along their chequebook!

MAKING A DIFFERENCE

When parents and grandparents stop you in the street or the school playground to tell you how much they enjoyed a performance, or how their child talks excitedly all week about the drama class, or how the child's play has become more imaginative, more focused and more fun since they began attending classes, you know that you are succeeding in your aims. When the children from your sessions happily dance up to you whenever they see you unexpectedly in another place and immediately initiate a conversation, you know that you have helped them to build the confidence and self-esteem that will benefit them throughout their lives.

If we can make drama accessible to everybody and give them the skills, the confidence, the social abilities and the enthusiasm to use it, we will contribute to making the world a better place for our children to grow up in – and how much more fun we will all have!

Index